SIDE BY SIDE
ACTIVITY WORKBOOK

1B

Steven J. Molinsky

Bill Bliss

Illustrated by

Richard E. Hill

Contributing Authors

Elizabeth Handley
Katharine Kolowich
with
Mary Ann Perry

Editorial Development

Tina B. Carver

Prentice-Hall, Inc., Englewood Cliffs, New Jersey 07632

Printed in the United States of America

11

ISBN 0-13-809582-5

Prentice-Hall International, Inc., *London*
Prentice-Hall of Australia Pty. Limited, *Sydney*
Editora Prentice-Hall do Brasil, Ltda., *Rio de Janeiro*
Prentice-Hall Canada Inc., *Toronto*
Prentice-Hall of India Private Limited, *New Delhi*
Prentice-Hall of Japan, Inc., *Tokyo*
Prentice-Hall of Southeast Asia Pte. Ltd., *Singapore*
Whitehall Books Limited, *Wellington, New Zealand*

Contents

18
Like To
Review of Tenses:
   Simple Present
   Simple Past
   Future: Going To
Indirect Object Pronouns   1

19
Count/Non-Count Nouns   8

20
Partitives
Count/Non-Count Nouns
Imperatives   16

21
Future Tense: Will
Prepositions of Time
Might   24

22
Comparatives
Should
Possessive Pronouns   31

23
Superlatives   41

24
Directions   49

25
Adverbs
Comparative of Adverbs
Agent Nouns
If-Clauses   55

26
Past Continuous Tense
Reflexive Pronouns
While-Clauses   64

27
Could
Be Able To
Have Got To
Too + Adjective   70

28
Must
Must vs. Should
Fewer/Less
Past Tense Review   78

29
Future Continuous Tense   84

30
Some/Any
Pronoun Review
Verb Tense Review   91

A. LIKES AND DISLIKES

bake	eat	study	visit	watch
dance	play	teach	wait for	write to

  like to / likes to

1. Alan ___*likes to play*___ chess.

2. Mrs. Johnson ___*doesn't like*___ ___*to teach.*___

don't like to / doesn't like to

3. Ted and Patty _____ ice cream.

4. Mr. and Mrs. Taylor _____ _____.

5. Susan _____ her grandparents.

6. David _____ _____.

7. We _____ TV together.

8. I _____.

9. Mary _____ her friends.

10. Mr. Jackson _____ _____ the train.

1

B. WRITE ABOUT YOURSELF

What do you like to do?

1. I like to . . . .

2. . . . .

3. . . . .

4. . . . .

5. . . . .

What don't you like to do?

1. I don't like to . . . .

2. . . . .

3. . . . .

4. . . . .

5. . . . .

C. DAY AFTER DAY

brush	clean	do	go	read	take	wash
buy	cry	get up	have	sing	talk	write

1. Tommy _talks_ to his girlfriend every evening.

Yesterday evening he _talked to his girlfriend._

Tomorrow evening _he's going to talk to his girlfriend._

2. Bobby and Billy _____ their bedroom every Saturday.

Last Saturday they _____ _____ .

Next Saturday _____ _____ .

3. Mr. Nelson _____ his car every Sunday.

Last Sunday he _____ _____ .

Next Sunday _____ _____ .

4. I _____ to my son every week.

Last week I _____ _____ .

Next week _____ _____ .

2

5. We _____ together every Sunday.

Last Sunday we _____

_____.

Next Sunday _____

_____.

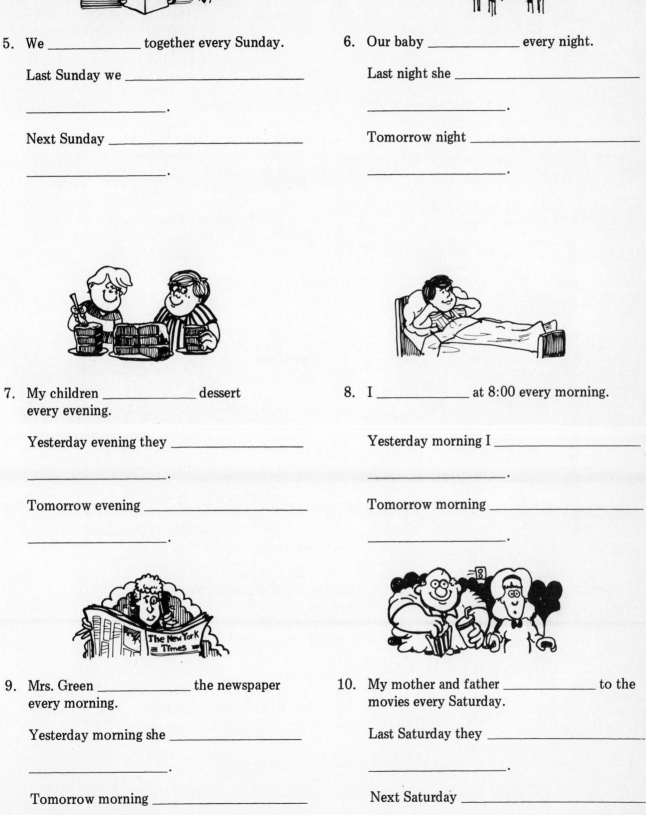

6. Our baby _____ every night.

Last night she _____

_____.

Tomorrow night _____

_____.

7. My children _____ dessert every evening.

Yesterday evening they _____

_____.

Tomorrow evening _____

_____.

8. I _____ at 8:00 every morning.

Yesterday morning I _____

_____.

Tomorrow morning _____

_____.

9. Mrs. Green _____ the newspaper every morning.

Yesterday morning she _____

_____.

Tomorrow morning _____

_____.

10. My mother and father _____ to the movies every Saturday.

Last Saturday they _____

_____.

Next Saturday _____

_____.

3

11. Robert _____ bananas every week.

Last week he _____

_____ .

Next week _____

_____ .

12. Our children _____ their teeth every morning.

Yesterday morning they _____

_____ .

Tomorrow morning _____

_____ .

13. Anna _____ the bus every morning.

Yesterday morning she _____

_____ .

Tomorrow morning _____

_____ .

14. My brother and I _____ our exercises every afternoon.

Yesterday afternoon we _____

_____ .

Tomorrow afternoon _____

_____ .

15. I . . . . every . . . .

Yesterday/Last . . . . I . . . .

Tomorrow/Next . . . .

D. WHAT'S JUDY GOING TO GIVE HER FAMILY?

Judy is looking for presents for her family.
Here's what she's going to give them.

1. Her brother George loves sports. _____ *She's going to give him a football.* _____

2. Her Aunt Betty likes to read. _____

3. Her cousins Peter and Nancy really like to eat. _____

4. Her daughter likes to listen to music. _____

5. Her son is never on time. _____

6. Her grandmother loves clothes. _____

7. Her father and mother like to travel. _____

8. Her grandfather loves pets. _____

E. PRESENTS

1. Last year I ___*gave*___ my husband a shirt.   This year ___*I'm going to give him*___ a tie.

2. Last year Mary _____ her sister a doll.   This year _____ a bracelet.

3. Last year Jack _____ his father a briefcase.   This year _____ an umbrella.

4. Last year Mr. Smith _____ his children a bird.   This year _____ a cat.

5. Last year Mr. and Mrs. Jones _____ their son a bicycle.   This year _____ clothes.

6. Last year Peter _____ his girlfriend a photograph.   This year _____ flowers.

7. Last year we _____ our mother and father candy.   This year _____ cookies.

8. Last year I . . . .   This year . . . .

. . . .

5

F.   LISTEN

Listen and write the correct activity under the appropriate date.

bowling	sailing	swimming
concert	football game	doctor
dentist	party	wedding

JULY

SUNDAY	MONDAY	TUESDAY	WEDNESDAY	THURSDAY	FRIDAY	SATURDAY
				1	2 bowling	3
4	5	6	7	8	9	10
11	12	13	14	15	16	17
18	19	20	21	22	23	24
25	26	27	28	29	30	31

G.   LISTEN

Listen and write the ordinal number you hear.

1. Peter Jones _____4th_____

2. the Smith family _____

3. The WHAMMO Company _____

4. Mary Nelson _____

5. drugstore _____

6. dentist's office _____

7. Barbara Harris and her son _____

8. Mr. and Mrs. Brown _____

9. Dr. Johnson _____

10. Mr. Jackson _____

11. Hilda Green _____

12. flower shop _____

13. Dr. Rinaldi _____

14. the Larson family _____

15. Mrs. Nathan _____

16. French restaurant _____

H. JOHNNY'S BIRTHDAYS

Fill in the missing words.

On Johnny's 7th birthday, his mother (take) _____took_____ him and his friends to the zoo.
1

After that, they all (go) _____ to a restaurant and (eat) _____ dessert. Johnny's friends
2   3

(love) _____ his birthday party, but Johnny was upset because his mother didn't (buy)
4

_____ him any candy at the zoo.
5

On Johnny's 10th birthday, he (have) _____ a picnic at the beach with his friends. They all
6

(play) _____ baseball and (go) _____ swimming. Johnny's friends
7   8

(love) _____ his birthday party, but Johnny was upset because he didn't (like)
9

_____ his presents. His friends (give) _____ him clothes and books, but Johnny
10   11

(want) _____ a football.
12

On Johnny's 13th birthday, he (have) _____ a party at home. His mother (cook)
13

_____ a big dinner, and his father (bake) _____ a cake. All his friends
14   15

(wish) _____ him "Happy Birthday." Johnny's friends (love) _____ his
16   17

birthday party, but Johnny was upset because the girls didn't (dance) _____. They
18

(sit) _____ and (talk) _____ and (watch) _____ TV.
19   20   21

On Johnny's 16th birthday, he didn't (have) _____ a party. He (go) _____
22   23

dancing with his girlfriend, and he (have) _____ a wonderful time. His friends didn't (give)
24

_____ him presents. His father didn't (bake) _____ him a cake. But Johnny
25   26

wasn't upset this time because his girlfriend (dance) _____ with him all night.
27

1. Why was Johnny upset on his 7th birthday? _____

_____

2. Why was he upset on his 10th birthday? _____

_____

3. Why was he upset on his 13th birthday? _____

_____

4. Was he upset on his 16th birthday? Why not? _____

_____

A. MISSING LABELS

Fill in the missing labels.

APPLES	BUTTER	EGGS	ONIONS
BANANAS	CHEESE	ICE CREAM	SODA
BREAD	COOKIES	MILK	SUGAR

1.

MILK

2.

_____

3.

4.

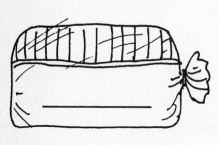

_____

5.

6.

7.

_____

8.

_____

9.

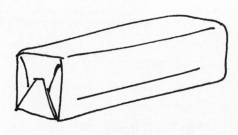

10.

_____

11.

12.

B. LOOKING FOR FOOD

there's	there are

1. _____There are_____ some onions, _____there's_____ some pepper, and _____ some bananas in Jeff's kitchen.

2. _____ some beer, _____ some butter, _____ some mayonnaise, _____ some tomatoes, _____ some milk, and _____ some apples in our refrigerator.

3. _____ some coffee, _____ some salt, and _____ some tea in Anita's kitchen.

4. _____ some ice cream and _____ some yogurt in Linda's refrigerator.

5. _____ some sugar and _____ some bread in Arthur's kitchen.

6. _____ some wine, _____ some eggs, _____ some lettuce, _____ some apples, _____ some melons, _____ some pears, and _____ some celery in Stanley's refrigerator.

7. _____ some soda, _____ some cheese, _____ some orange juice, _____ some jam, and _____ some jelly in Barbara's refrigerator.

C. I'M SORRY, BUT . . .

Look at the menu to see what Ed's Restaurant has and doesn't have today.

1.
May I have some chicken and beans?

I'm sorry, but _____ *there aren't*

_____ *any beans.*

2.
May I have a pizza and some beer?

I'm sorry, but _____ *there isn't*

_____ *any beer.*

3.
May I have some yogurt and some tea?

I'm sorry, but _____

_____.

4.
May I have a salad and some lemonade?

I'm sorry, but _____

_____.

5.
May I have some chicken and french fries?

I'm sorry, but _____

_____.

6.
May I have some cake and ice cream?

I'm sorry, but _____

_____.

7.
May I have some cookies and milk?

I'm sorry, but _____

_____.

8.
May I have some cheese and wine?

I'm sorry, but _____

_____.

9.
May I have some bread and jam?

I'm sorry, but _____

_____.

10.
May I have some cheese and crackers?

I'm sorry, but _____

_____.

10

D.   LISTEN: *"I'M SORRY, BUT THERE _____ ANY."*

Listen and put a circle around the correct word.

1. (isn't) / aren't	5. isn't / aren't	9. isn't / aren't	13. isn't / aren't
2. isn't / aren't	6. isn't / aren't	10. isn't / aren't	14. isn't / aren't
3. isn't / aren't	7. isn't / aren't	11. isn't / aren't	15. isn't / aren't
4. isn't / aren't	8. isn't / aren't	12. isn't / aren't	16. isn't / aren't

E.   **WHAT DO YOU WANT TO EAT?**

1. There _____ *aren't any eggs.* _____

    How about some _____ *cereal?* _____

2. There _____ *isn't any chicken.* _____

    How about some _____?

3. There _____.

    How about some _____?

4. There _____.

    How about some _____?

5. There _____.

    How about some _____?

6. There _____.

    How about some _____?

11

7. There _____.

   How about some _____?

8. There _____.

   How about some _____?

F.   HOME FROM VACATION

The Jackson family got home this morning from their vacation. They had a wonderful time, but they aren't feeling very well today. Why not?

What's the matter with Mr. Jackson? Last night he went to an expensive restaurant with his family, and he ate too ⊙much / many dessert. He ate so much / many dessert that he's in bed today with a stomachache.

Why do Alice and Jane Jackson feel terrible? At the restaurant last night, Jane ate too much / many garlic and too much / many onions, and Alice ate too much / many bread. Alice ate so much / many bread that she can't wear the new clothes she bought on vacation. When she put on her new skirt this morning, it was too small.

Mrs. Jackson and her son Robert didn't eat too much / many food last night, but they don't feel very well either. Mrs. Jackson is tired because she visited too much / many churches and monuments yesterday, and she went to too much / many stores. Robert is tired because he wrote letters all morning and all afternoon on his last day of vacation. He wrote so much / many letters that he's never going to write a letter again.

What's the matter with John Jackson? He feels terrible because he drank too [much / many] wine, and he smoked too [much / many] cigarettes last night. He drank so [much / many] wine, and he smoked so [much / many] cigarettes that he has a bad headache today.

Why does Linda Jackson look upset? She's depressed because she bought too [much / many] expensive presents. She bought so [much / many] presents that she's going to have to work every day after school this month.

1. How [**much** / many] dessert did Mr. Jackson eat? _____ *He ate so much dessert that he's* _____

_____ *in bed today with a stomachache.* _____

2. How [much / many] bread did Alice eat? _____

_____

3. How [much / many] letters did Robert write? _____

_____

4. How [much / many] wine did John drink? _____

_____

5. How [much / many] presents did Linda buy? _____

_____

9.

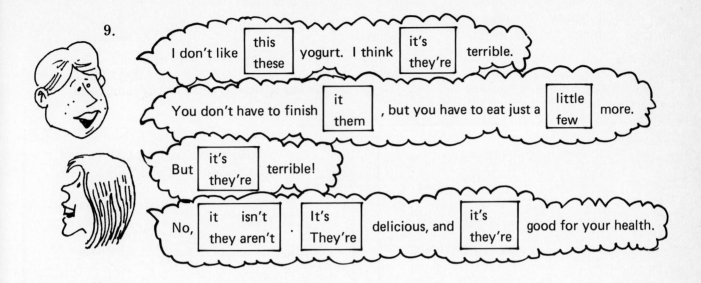

H. LISTEN

Listen and put a √ next to the correct picture.

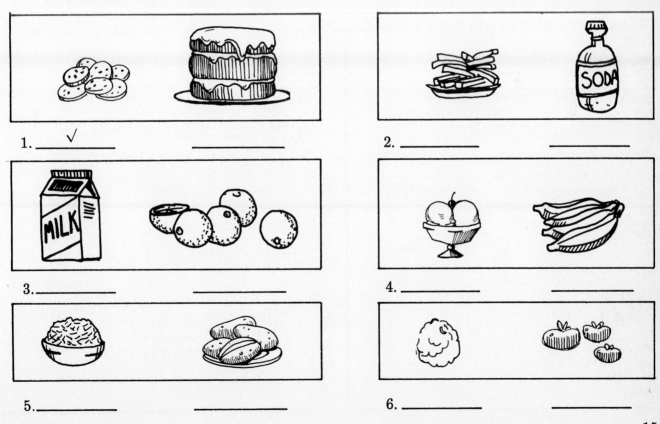

1. _____ √ _____   _____   2. _____   _____

3. _____   _____   4. _____   _____

5. _____   _____   6. _____   _____

15

A. SHOPPING LISTS

bag	bunch	head	loaf/loaves	of
bottle	can	jar	pack	
box	dozen	lb. (pound)	quart	

1. Mary's friend is going to visit this afternoon.

Mary's Shopping List

a _____ *bottle* _____ *of* soda

a _____ _____ cookies

a _____ _____ bread

a _____ _____ butter

a _____ _____ jam

2. Robert's friend is going to have lunch with him.

Robert's Shopping List

a _____ _____ milk

a _____ _____ eggs

½ _____ _____ cheese

a _____ _____ beans

a _____ _____ lettuce

a _____ _____ carrots

3. Jack is going to have a party tonight.

Jack's Shopping List

2 _____ _____ wine

10 _____ _____ beer

1 _____ _____ cigarettes

2 _____ _____ crackers

a _____ _____ cheese

a _____ _____ coffee

3 _____ _____ bananas

4. Eleanor is going to make a big lunch for her friends.

Eleanor's Shopping List

a _____ _____ flour

a _____ _____ eggs

a _____ _____ sugar

a _____ _____ butter

a _____ _____ apples

2 _____ _____ bread

a _____ _____ mayonnaise

2 _____ _____ lettuce

2 _____ _____ carrots

3 _____ _____ wine

5. You're going to make a big dinner for your classmates. What are you going to buy?

My Shopping List

....
....
....
....
....
....
....

B. LISTEN

Listen and write the prices you hear.

1. _____*35¢*_____

2. _____*$1.40*_____

3. _____

4. _____

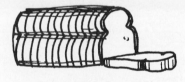

5. _____

6. _____

7. _____

8. _____

9. _____

10. _____

11. _____

12. _____

C. SHOPPING FOR FOOD

apples	bread	costs	loaf	much	quart
are	bunch	does	loaves	of	
bananas	cost	is	milk	pound	

1.

How _____much_____ does a _____bunch_____ of bananas _____cost?_____

A _____ of _____ _____ a dollar ten.

Are you sure? That's a lot _____ money!

I know. Bananas _____ very expensive this week.

2.

How _____ does a _____ of milk _____?

A _____ of milk _____ seventy-nine cents.

SEVENTY-NINE CENTS?! That's terrible!

I'm sorry. _____ _____ very expensive this week.

3.

How _____ _____ a _____ of bread _____?

A _____ of _____ _____ forty-five cents.

That's wonderful! May I have ten _____, please.

Ten _____?! That's a lot _____ bread!

You're right. But _____ _____ very cheap this week.

4. May I help you?

Yes, please. How _____ _____ a _____ _____ apples

_____?

A _____ of _____ _____ a dollar thirty.

A DOLLAR THIRTY?! That's too _____ money!

I'm sorry. _____ _____ expensive today, but oranges _____

very cheap. You can buy a _____ of oranges for just forty cents.

That's nice! But how can I make an apple pie with oranges?!

D. WHERE WOULD YOU LIKE TO GO FOR LUNCH?

are	cups	is	much	piece
bowl	dish	it	of	they
coffee	glass	many	order	

A. Where would you like to go for lunch?

B. Let's go to Henry's Restaurant. Their pancakes __*are*__₁ fantastic, and _____₂ aren't expensive. I had an _____₃ _____₄ pancakes there last Saturday for a dollar fifty.

A. I don't want to go to Henry's Restaurant. Their pancakes _____₅ O.K., but you can't get any beer. I like to have a _____₆ _____₇ beer with my lunch.

B. How about Tom's Restaurant? Their soup _____₈ excellent, and _____₉ isn't expensive. A _____₁₀ _____₁₁ soup costs fifty-nine cents.

A. I really don't like Tom's Restaurant. The soup _____₁₂ good, but their salad _____₁₃ terrible. _____₁₄ has too _____₁₅ lettuce and too _____₁₆ onions.

B. How about Mario's Restaurant? Their desserts are wonderful. You can get a _____₁₇ _____₁₈ apple pie, a _____₁₉ _____₂₀ ice cream, or a _____₂₁ _____₂₂ strawberries.

A. I know, but their coffee _____₂₃ terrible. I like to have two or three _____₂₄ _____₂₅ _____₂₆ with my dessert.

B. Wait a minute! I know where we can go for lunch. Let's go to YOUR house!

A. That's a good idea.

E.   LISTEN: *WHAT DID THEY HAVE?*

Listen and write the missing words.

1. David usually has two ____bowls____ __of__ cereal for breakfast. This morning he got up late and

    had a _____ of _____ .

2. Jane usually has a _____ _____ orange juice with her lunch. Yesterday was her birthday,

    and she had two _____ of _____ .

3. Mr. Nelson usually has two _____ of _____ with his dinner. Yesterday he

    visited his Japanese neighbors and had a _____ _____ _____ .

4. Peter usually has a _____ of _____ for lunch. Yesterday he was very hungry, and he

    had three _____ _____ chicken.

5. Lois usually has a _____ _____ yogurt for lunch. This afternoon she went to a restaurant

    and had two _____ _____ french fries.

6. Marie usually has a _____ of _____ for dessert. Yesterday she went to a party and

    had three _____ _____ ice cream.

7. Alice usually has a _____ _____ hot chocolate for breakfast. Yesterday morning she went to a

    restaurant and had an _____ of _____ .

8. Nancy usually has a _____ of _____ for dessert. Yesterday she visited her

    grandmother and had two _____ of _____ and a _____ _____ strawberries.

F.   BETTY'S DELICIOUS STEW

Put a circle around the correct words.

A.   How do you make your delicious stew, Betty?

B.   It's very easy. First I put a (little) / few butter into a pan. Then I chop up a little / few onions and

a little / few garlic. After that, I cut up some chicken, and I add a little / few salt and a little / few

pepper. Then I cut up a little / few tomatoes, and I slice a little / few mushrooms. Then I pour in a

cup of wine and a little / few chicken soup. I cook the stew for an hour.

Betty's Recipe for Stew

1. _____*Put a little*_____ butter into a pan.

2. _____ onions and

   _____ garlic.

3. _____ some chicken.

4. _____ salt and _____ pepper.

5. _____ tomatoes.

6. _____ mushrooms.

7. _____ wine and

   _____ chicken soup.

8. _____ for an hour.

CHECK-UP TEST: Chapters 18-20

A. Put a circle around the correct word.

Ex. Cheese (is)/are expensive this week.

1. My dentist says I eat too much/many cookies.

2. She ate so much/many ice cream that she's

    going to have a stomachache tomorrow.

3. Would you care for a little/few beans?

    I bought it/them this morning and it's/they're

    very fresh.

4. This/These rice is/are delicious. May I have

    a little/few more?

5. How much/many does a pound of apples cost?

B. Fill in the blanks.

Ex. a ___quart___ of

    . ___milk___

1. a _____ of

    _____

2. a _____ of

    _____

3. a _____ of

    _____

4. 2 _____ of

    _____

5. 2 _____ of

    _____

6. 2 _____ of

    _____

C. Complete the sentences.

Ex. Jane cooks spaghetti every week.

    Last week ___she cooked___ spaghetti.

    Next week ___she's going to cook___ spaghetti.

1. Johnny watches TV every evening.

    Yesterday evening he _____
    TV.

    Tomorrow evening _____
    TV.

2. I talk on the telephone every day.

    Yesterday I _____
    on the telephone.

    Tomorrow _____
    on the telephone.

22

3. Ed drinks coffee every morning.

    Yesterday morning he _____ coffee.

    Tomorrow morning _____ coffee.

4. We write to our uncle every week.

    Last week we _____ to our uncle.

    Next week _____ to our uncle.

5. Judy and Sara have a big birthday party every year.

    Last year they _____ a big birthday party.

    Next year _____ a big party.

6. We go skiing every winter.

    Last winter we _____ skiing.

    Next winter _____ skiing.

D. Complete the sentences.

Ex. Last year I gave my sister a necklace for her birthday.

    This year _____*I'm going to give her*_____ earrings.

1. Last year we gave our neighbors flowers.

    This year _____ candy.

2. Last year Mary gave her father a record.

    This year _____ a briefcase.

3. Last year Billy gave his mother a book.

    This year _____ perfume.

E. Listen and put a circle around the correct word.

    "I'm sorry, but there _____ any."

Ex. (isn't)
     aren't

1. isn't
    aren't

2. isn't
    aren't

3. isn't
    aren't

4. isn't
    aren't

5. isn't
    aren't

A. SOON

21

1. Will the movie begin soon?

Yes, _____*it will.*_____ _____*It'll*_____

_____*begin*_____ in a few minutes.

2. Will Uncle Albert be here soon?

Yes, _____. _____

_____ in a little while.

3. Will Mr. and Mrs. Smith leave soon?

Yes, _____. _____

_____ in an hour.

4. _____ your mother _____ soon?

Yes, _____. _____ get up in a little while.

5. _____ dinner _____ soon?

Yes, _____. _____ be ready in a few minutes.

6. Will you _____ your homework soon?

Yes, _____. _____ finish it in an hour.

7. _____ Mary and Bob _____ _____ soon?

Yes, _____. _____ get married next month.

8. _____ you _____ soon?

Yes, _____. _____ get out of the hospital in a few days.

B. WHAT DO YOU THINK?

		YES!	NO!

1. What will Mary study next year?

Maybe _____ *she'll* _____ *study* _____ French.

I'm sure _____ *she* _____ *won't study* Spanish.

2. When will Billy call his uncle?

Maybe _____ him tomorrow.

I'm sure _____ _____ him tonight.

3. What will your children have for dessert?

Maybe _____ some ice cream.

I'm sure _____ _____ any pie.

4. Where will you and Sally go this evening?

Maybe _____ _____ to a concert.

I'm sure _____ _____ to a movie again.

5. Where will George live next year?

Maybe _____ in New York.

I'm sure _____ _____ at home.

6. Do you think it'll be cold tomorrow?

Maybe _____ cold.

I'm sure _____ _____ hot.

7. When will you finish your homework?

Maybe _____ it tomorrow.

I'm sure _____ _____ it tonight.

8. Who will Jane go out with on Saturday?

Maybe _____ _____ with Robert.

I'm sure _____ _____ with Fred.

9. What do you think you'll get for your birthday?

Maybe _____ some books.

I'm sure _____ _____ clothes.

10. What will Mr. and Mrs. Peterson plant in their garden?

Maybe _____ _____ tomatoes.

I'm sure _____ _____ flowers.

11. When will the train arrive?

Maybe _____ in half an hour.

I'm sure _____ _____ on time.

12. When will Mr. and Mrs. Smith move to Miami?

Maybe _____ there in ten years.

I'm sure _____ _____ there soon.

13. When will we finish our English book?

Maybe _____ it in a few months.

I'm sure _____ _____ it very soon.

C. WRITE AND SAY IT

Write and say the sentences.

he'll	she'll
it'll	they'll

1. Mary thinks the school bus will arrive at 3:00.

   Her husband thinks _____ *it'll arrive* _____ at 4:00.

2. Mary thinks Uncle Harry will call tonight.

   Her husband thinks _____ tomorrow.

3. Mary thinks her neighbors will move to New York.

   Her husband thinks _____ to Boston.

4. Mary thinks their daughter will be an actress

   Her husband thinks _____ a violinist.

5. Mary thinks the children will be home soon.

   Her husband thinks _____ late again.

6. Mary thinks the car will be ready today.

   Her husband thinks _____ next week.

D. LISTEN

Listen and put a circle around the words you hear.

1. won't / (want to)

5. won't / want to

9. won't / want to

13. won't / want to

2. won't / want to

6. won't / want to

10. won't / want to

14. won't / want to

3. won't / want to

7. won't / want to

11. won't / want to

15. won't / want to

4. won't / want to

8. won't / want to

12. won't / want to

E. WE DON'T KNOW

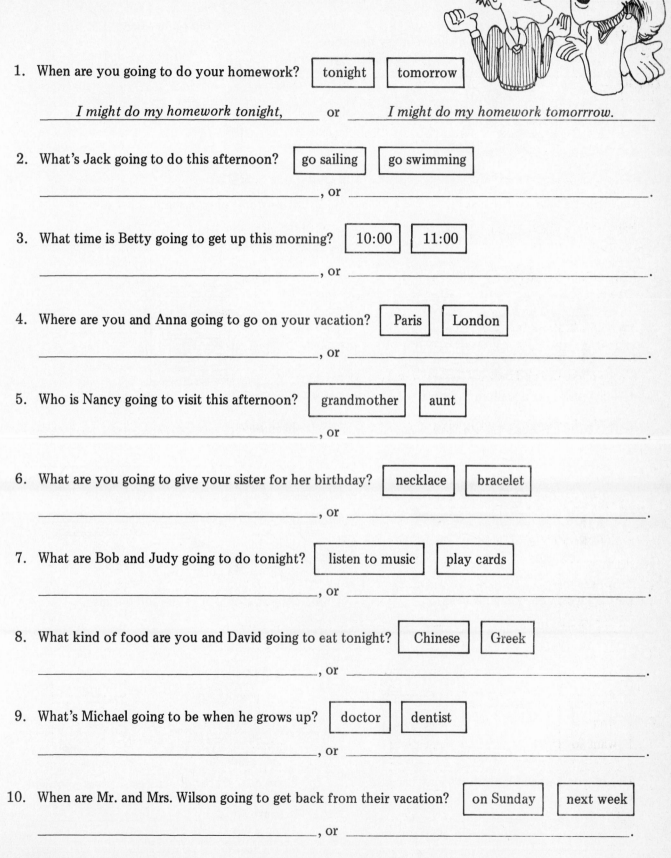

1. When are you going to do your homework? [tonight] [tomorrow]

    _____ *I might do my homework tonight,* _____ or _____ *I might do my homework tomorrrow.* _____

2. What's Jack going to do this afternoon? [go sailing] [go swimming]

    _____, or _____.

3. What time is Betty going to get up this morning? [10:00] [11:00]

    _____, or _____.

4. Where are you and Anna going to go on your vacation? [Paris] [London]

    _____, or _____.

5. Who is Nancy going to visit this afternoon? [grandmother] [aunt]

    _____, or _____.

6. What are you going to give your sister for her birthday? [necklace] [bracelet]

    _____, or _____.

7. What are Bob and Judy going to do tonight? [listen to music] [play cards]

    _____, or _____.

8. What kind of food are you and David going to eat tonight? [Chinese] [Greek]

    _____, or _____.

9. What's Michael going to be when he grows up? [doctor] [dentist]

    _____, or _____.

10. When are Mr. and Mrs. Wilson going to get back from their vacation? [on Sunday] [next week]

    _____, or _____.

F. THE PESSIMISTS

break her leg	get fat	look terrible
catch a cold	get home very late	miss their train
fall asleep	get seasick	rain
get a backache	go to jail	step on her feet
get a sunburn	have noisy neighbors	
get drunk	have too much homework	

1. Jack won't go sailing because

    _____
    he's afraid he might

    _____
    get seasick.

2. Tom won't play basketball because

    _____

    _____.

3. Helen won't take a walk in the park because

    _____

    _____.

4. We won't live in an apartment building

    because _____

    _____.

 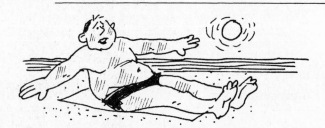

5. Barbara won't go skiing because

    _____

    _____.

6. Albert won't sit in the sun because

    _____

    _____.

7. Steven won't wash his clothes today because

    _____

    _____.

8. George won't drink wine at the party tonight

    because _____

    _____.

28

9. Jennifer won't take English next year in

school because _____

_____ .

10. Fred won't eat any dessert because

_____

_____ .

11. George and his brother won't have lunch with

us this afternoon because _____

_____

_____ .

12. Jim won't go dancing with Patty because

_____

_____

_____ .

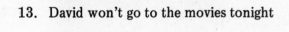

13. David won't go to the movies tonight

because _____

_____ .

14. Frank won't get a haircut because

_____

_____ .

15. Ronald won't go to Peggy's party this

Saturday night because _____

_____ .

16. I won't steal cars anymore because

_____

_____ .

W!

Fill in the words; then read the sentences aloud.

warm	wearing	Williams	winter

1. Mrs. _____*Williams*_____ is _____*wearing*_____

a _____*warm*_____ _____*winter*_____ coat.

wedding	wine	won't	worry

2. Don't _____! I _____

drink too much _____ at

the _____.

wasn't	Wednesday	well	William

3. _____ _____

at work on _____

because he didn't feel _____.

washing	we're	WHAMMO
windows	with	

4. _____ _____ our

_____ _____

_____ Window Cleaner.

wait	Walter	war	wife	will

5. _____ will fight in the

_____. Walter's _____

_____ have to _____

at home.

swimming	wanted	warm	wasn't
we	weather		

6. _____ _____ to go

_____, but the

_____ _____

_____.

A. OLD AND NEW

1. My old house was large. My new house is _____ *larger.* _____

2. Linda's old car was fast. Her new car is _____.

3. My old sofa was soft. My new sofa is _____.

4. Our old apartment building was clean. Our new apartment building is _____.

5. Our old dishes were shiny. Our new dishes are _____.

6. Mrs. Black's old hat was fancy. Her new hat is _____.

7. My old neighbors were friendly. My new neighbors are _____.

8. Jane's old school was big. Her new school is _____.

9. Shirley's old bicycle was safe. Her new bicycle is _____.

10. Jack's old watch was cheap. His new watch is _____.

11. My old earrings were pretty. My new earrings are _____.

12. Walter's old job was easy. His new job is _____.

13. Billy's old mittens were warm. His new mittens are _____.

14. Jeff's old records were noisy. His new records are _____.

15. Sara's old coat was heavy. Her new coat is _____.

16. Helen's old neighborhood was quiet. Her new neighborhood is _____.

17. Our old doctor was always busy. Our new doctor is _____.

18. Dan's old shirt was white. His new shirt is _____.

19. Rita's old cat was always hungry. Her new cat is _____.

20. My old English book was short. My new English book is _____.

21. Fred's old dog was fat. His new dog is _____.

B. THEY'RE DIFFERENT

1. My uncle is energetic, but my cousin is _____ *more energetic.* _____

2. Mrs. Smith's apple pie is delicious, but my mother's apple pie is _____.

3. My brother is intelligent, but his girlfriend is _____.

4. Our furniture is comfortable, but our neighbor's furniture is _____.

5. Mary's husband is handsome, but her son is _____.

6. My children are lazy, but my sister's children are _____.

7. Uncle Albert is poor, but Uncle Edward is _____.

8. Herman is hungry, but Harry is _____.

9. Sally's apartment is attractive, but George's apartment is _____.

10. David's watch is accurate, but his teacher's watch is _____.

11. My suitcase is light, but my brother's suitcase is _____.

12. Our stove is dirty, but our neighbor's stove is _____.

13. Paul's teeth are white, but his dentist's teeth are _____.

14. My pet bird is beautiful, but Betty's bird is _____.

15. Tommy's hair is short, but his barber's hair is _____.

16. Aunt Mary is old, but Uncle Bob is _____.

17. Yesterday was hot, but today is _____.

18. Henry is thin, but his girlfriend is _____.

19. Bill's clothes are expensive, but his roommate's clothes are _____.

20. My children are healthy, but my doctor's children are _____.

21. My feet are large, but my father's feet are _____.

C. WHAT SHOULD THEY DO?

buy new clothes	call the police	get a wig	go to the doctor
call a mechanic	drink tea	go on vacation	move to a
call the plumber	get a job	go to the dentist	new apartment

1. The sink in Walter's bathroom is broken. What should he do?

   He should call the plumber.

2. Mary has a toothache. What should she do?

   _____

3. Mr. and Mrs. Smith don't like their new apartment building. What should they do?

   _____

4. Mr. Jones worked every day this year, and he's very tired. What should he do?

   _____

5. Billy is much bigger this year. His old clothes are too small. What should he do?

   _____

6. Doris has a headache and a stomachache. What should she do?

   _____

7. Jack's car is broken, and he can't fix it. What should he do?

   _____

8. My doctor says coffee isn't good for my health. What should I do?

   _____

9. A thief stole Mr. and Mrs. Johnson's car. What should they do?

   _____

10. Martha wants to buy a motorcycle, but she doesn't have much money. What should she do?

    _____

11. I think my hair looks terrible. What should I do?

    _____

33

D. PUZZLE

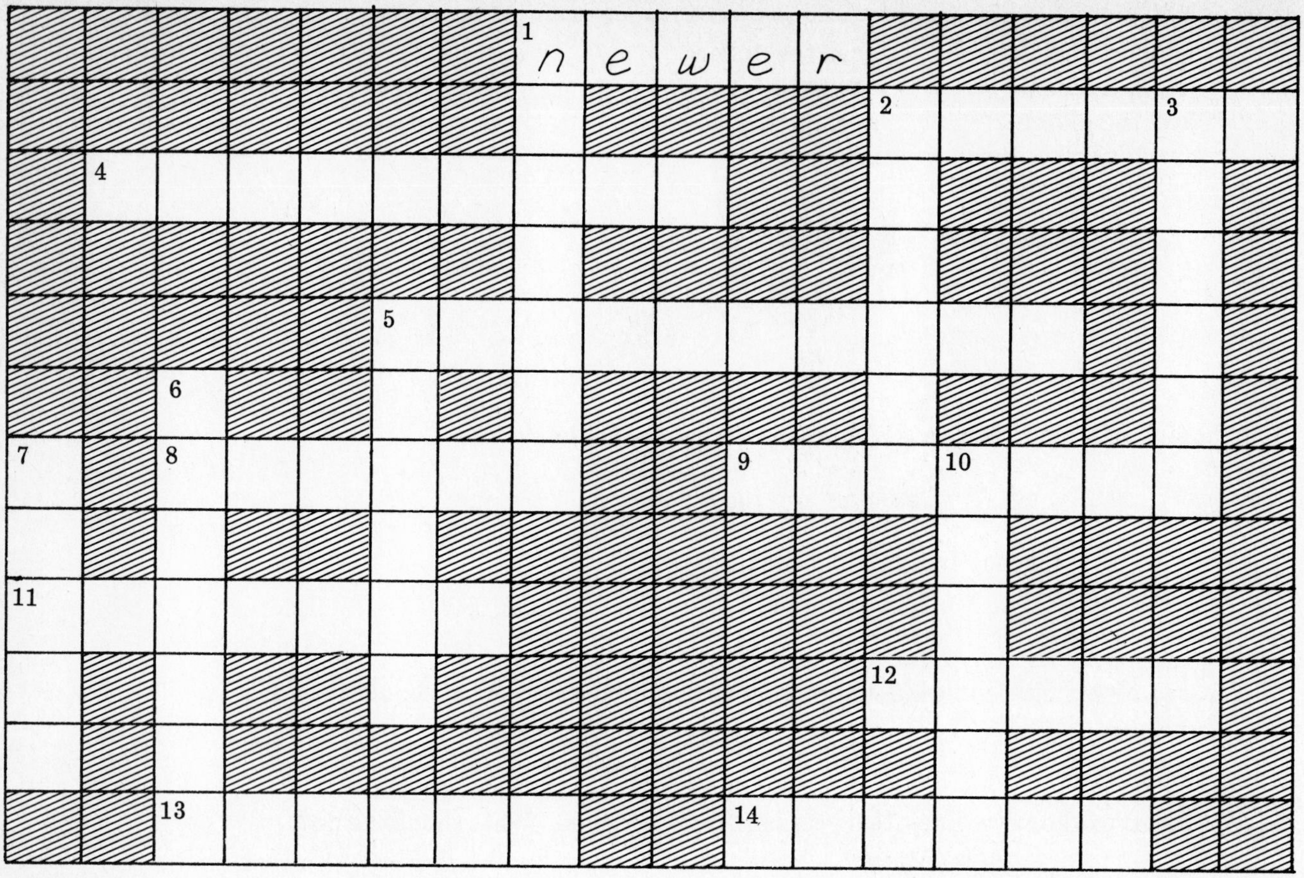

The crossword grid shows 1 Across filled in: **n e w e r**

Across

1. John's car is older than Helen's car. Helen's car is _____ than John's car.
2. Our kitchen is smaller than our bedroom. Our bedroom is _____ than our kitchen.
4. Barbara is always sick. Frieda is never sick. Frieda is _____ than Barbara.
5. Dogs really like to be with people. They're _____ than cats.
8. Yesterday was 95°F. Today is 90°F. Yesterday was _____ than today.
9. We cleaned our apartment today. Yesterday our apartment was _____.
11. Mario's Restaurant is fancy, but Pierre's Restaurant is _____.
12. My sister is younger than I am. I'm _____ than my sister.
13. Peter has a lot of money. He's _____ than his friends.
14. Peter's friends don't have much money. They're _____ than Peter.

Down

1. Ted is quieter than Walter. Walter is _____ than Ted.
2. George works every day. Mark rarely works. Mark is _____ than George.
3. Lesson 21 is more difficult than Lesson 20. Lesson 20 is _____ than Lesson 21.
5. Jack eats too much cake and candy. That's why he's _____ than his brothers.
6. Anita put WHAMMO Floor Wax on her floor yesterday, and now it's _____ than before.
7. William always travels by train because he thinks trains are _____ than planes.
10. Last year Tommy was short, but this year he's _____.

34

E. YOU DECIDE

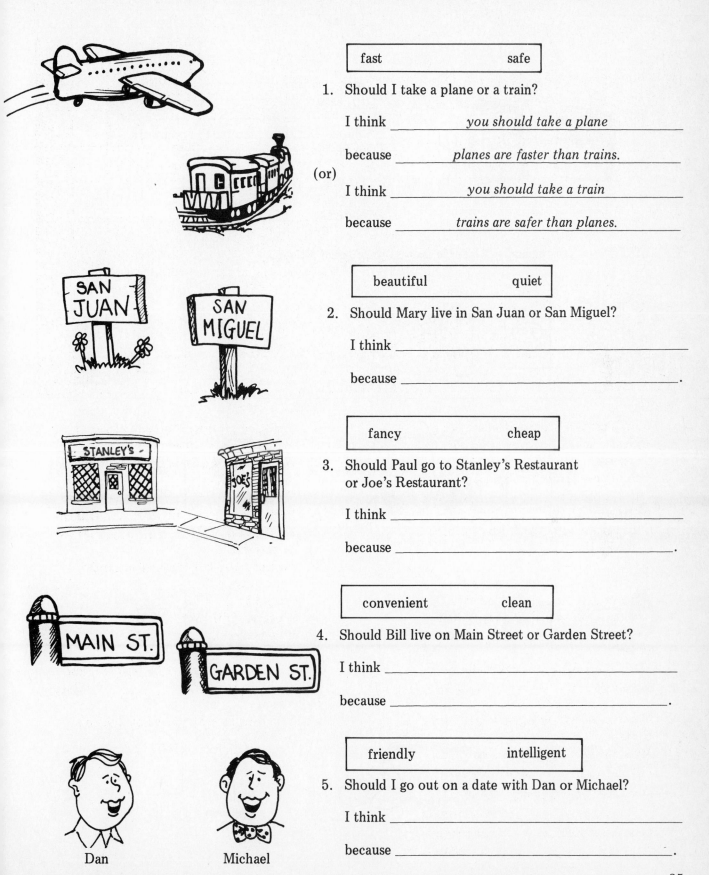

fast	safe

1. Should I take a plane or a train?

   I think _____*you should take a plane*_____

   because _____*planes are faster than trains.*_____

(or)

   I think _____*you should take a train*_____

   because _____*trains are safer than planes.*_____

beautiful	quiet

2. Should Mary live in San Juan or San Miguel?

   I think _____

   because _____.

fancy	cheap

3. Should Paul go to Stanley's Restaurant or Joe's Restaurant?

   I think _____

   because _____.

convenient	clean

4. Should Bill live on Main Street or Garden Street?

   I think _____

   because _____.

friendly	intelligent

5. Should I go out on a date with Dan or Michael?

   I think _____

   because _____.

Dan   Michael

warm	attractive

6. Should Judy buy mittens or gloves?

I think _____

because _____.

easy	interesting

7. Should David do his French homework
   or his mathematics homework?

I think _____

because _____.

F.   LISTEN   Listen and put a circle around the correct answer.

1.   George   Jennifer

2.   Albert   John

3.   Ted's dog   Fred and Sally's dog

4.   Robert   Nancy

5.   English test   French test

6.   Alice   Margaret

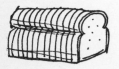

7.   85¢   80¢

8.   Bob   Bill

G. WHAT'S THE WORD?

mine	ours
his	yours
hers	theirs

1. Is that John's bicycle?
   No, it isn't _____ *his.* _____

2. Is that Mr. and Mrs. Smith's car?
   No, it isn't _____.

3. Are those your mother's earrings?
   No, they aren't _____.

4. Is that my recipe for vegetable soup?
   No, it isn't _____.

5. Are these Johnny's shoes?
   No, they aren't _____.

6. Are these Maria's cigarettes?
   No, they aren't _____.

7. Is that your dog?
   No, it isn't _____.

H. DIFFERENT, BUT O.K.

1. John (rich) _____ *isn't as rich as* _____ Tom, but he's much (happy) _____ *happier.* _____

2. Our apartment (clean) _____ Rita's apartment, but it's much

   (comfortable) _____.

3. Linda's children (intelligent) _____ Maria's children, but

   they're much (healthy) _____.

4. My room (large) _____ my sister's room, but it's much

   (pretty) _____.

5. Our neighborhood (safe) _____ Steve's neighborhood, but it's

   much (interesting) _____.

6. George's dog (smart) _____ Fred's dog, but it's much

   (friendly) _____.

7. Walter (handsome) _____ Tim, but he's much (nice)

   _____.

8. My watch (accurate) _____ Jennifer's watch, but it's much

(cheap) _____.

9. Betty's car (new) _____ Carol's car, but it's much (shiny)

_____.

10. Mrs. Green (young) _____ Sally, but she's much (energetic)

_____.

11. This rug (expensive) _____ Bob's rug, but it's much

(soft) _____.

12. Ed's car (big) _____ Jeff's car, but it's much (good)

_____.

I.   YOU'RE RIGHT

1. Peggy isn't as talented as Ginger.

You're right. Ginger is ___*more*___

_____*talented than*_____ Peggy.

2. English isn't as difficult as Arabic.

You're right. Arabic is _____

_____ English.

3. Dr. Smith isn't as busy as Dr. Brown.

You're right. Dr. Brown is _____

_____ Dr. Smith.

4. Toronto isn't _____ Mexico City.

You're right. Mexico City is noisier than Toronto.

5. Bill's apartment isn't _____

_____ Roger's apartment.

You're right. Roger's apartment is bigger than Bill's apartment.

6. Betty isn't as beautiful as her mother.

You're right. Betty's mother is

_____ Betty.

7. My suitcase isn't _____

_____ yours.

You're right. Your suitcase is heavier than mine.

8. Miguel isn't _____ Carlos.

You're right. Carlos is nicer than Miguel.

J.   WHO SHOULD WE HIRE?

Fill in the missing words.

A.   Do you think we should hire Miss Jackson? Everybody says she's capable and honest.

B.   I know. Miss Jackson is very honest, but how about Mrs. Wilson? I think she's (interesting)

_____*more interesting*_____ than Miss Jackson, and she's much (smart) _____.
        1   2

A.   I agree. Mrs. Wilson is very intelligent, but in my opinion she isn't as (smart) _____
                                                                                               3

as Mr. Brown. Maybe we should give Mr. Brown the job.

B.   No. I really don't think so. Mr. Brown is (lively) _____ than Miss
                                                                4

Jackson, but he isn't as (capable) _____ as Mrs. Wilson. You know, I think
                                              5

Mr. Smith is the right person for the job. He's (talented) _____
                                                                                    6

than Miss Jackson, he's (polite) _____ than Mr. Brown, and
                                                  7

he's (friendly) _____ than Mrs. Wilson.
                          8

A.   Do you think he's as (intelligent) _____ as Mr. Brown?
                                                9

B.   I think so. And he isn't as (talkative) _____.
                                                    10

A.   You're right. He's (good) _____ for the job than Miss Jackson, Mrs. Wilson, or
                                        11

Mr. Brown. Let's hire him!

K. DO YOU AGREE?

> I agree.
> I disagree.
> I agree/disagree with
>   (you, him, her, John . . .).
>
> I think so.
> I don't think so.
> In my opinion, . . .

Tom:

> I think Chinese food is more delicious than Italian food.

George:

> I disagree with you. I think Italian food is much more delicious than Chinese food.

1. What's Tom's opinion? _____

2. Does George agree? _____

3. Do YOU agree with Tom or with George? Why? . . . .

. . . .

Anita:

> I think dogs are smarter than cats.

Edward:

> I don't think so. In my opinion, cats are much smarter than dogs.

4. Does Edward agree with Anita? _____

5. What's Edward's opinion? _____

6. What's YOUR opinion?. . . . .

. . . .

Robert:

> In my opinion, English is more useful than Latin.

Anna:

> I disagree. I think Latin is more useful than English.

Miguel:

> I agree with Robert.

7. What does Robert think? _____

8. Does Anna agree with him? _____

9. What does Miguel think? _____

10. What do YOU think? Why? . . . .

. . . .

A. WHAT DO YOU THINK?

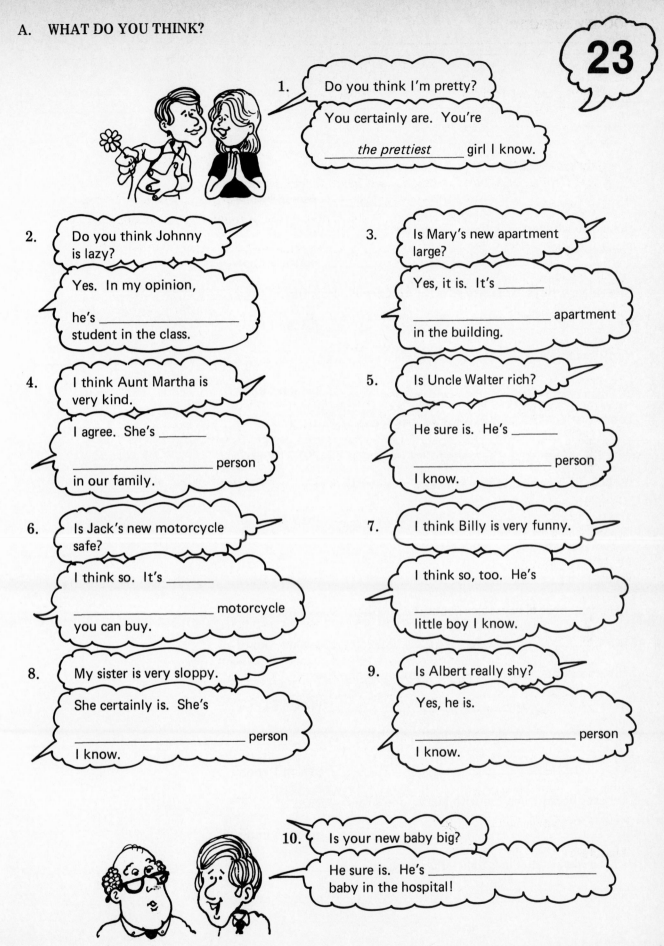

23

1. Do you think I'm pretty?

You certainly are. You're

_____the prettiest_____ girl I know.

2. Do you think Johnny is lazy?

Yes. In my opinion,

he's _____ student in the class.

3. Is Mary's new apartment large?

Yes, it is. It's _____

_____ apartment in the building.

4. I think Aunt Martha is very kind.

I agree. She's _____

_____ person in our family.

5. Is Uncle Walter rich?

He sure is. He's _____

_____ person I know.

6. Is Jack's new motorcycle safe?

I think so. It's _____

_____ motorcycle you can buy.

7. I think Billy is very funny.

I think so, too. He's

_____ little boy I know.

8. My sister is very sloppy.

She certainly is. She's

_____ person I know.

9. Is Albert really shy?

Yes, he is.

_____ person I know.

10. Is your new baby big?

He sure is. He's _____ baby in the hospital!

41

B.   WHAT'S THE WORD?

boring	energetic	honest	lazy	polite	stubborn
bright	generous	interesting	patient	stingy	talented

1. Steve always says "thank you." He's very _____ *polite.*

   He's _____ *the most polite* _____ person I know.

2. Helen is a wonderful violinist. She's very _____.

   She's _____ person I know.

3. Peter always buys expensive gifts for his friends. He's very _____.

   He's _____ person I know.

4. Harry swims every day before work. He's very _____.

   He's _____ person I know.

5. Tom never does his homework. He's very _____.

   He's _____ boy I know.

6. My boss never wants to give me more money. He's very _____.

   He's _____ person I know.

7. Betty never gets angry. She's very _____.

   She's _____ person I know.

8. My cousin Alice always talks about the weather. She's very _____.

   She's _____ person I know.

9. Sally knows the answers to all the questions. She's very _____.

   She's _____ person I know.

10. Uncle Robert always says what he thinks. He's very _____.

    He's _____ person I know.

11. I'm never bored when I'm with Mary. She's very _____.

    She's _____ person I know.

12. Henry is always sure he's right. He's very _____.

    He's _____ person I know.

C. AROUND THE WORLD

Gloria Green is the wealthiest woman in Centerville. She loves to go shopping. Last year she traveled around the world and bought presents for all her friends and family.

1. (attractive)   She bought a pocketbook in Rome because she thinks Italian pocketbooks are

   _____*the most attractive*_____ pocketbooks in the world.

2. (soft)   She bought leather gloves in Madrid because she thinks Spanish gloves are

   _____ gloves in the world.

3. (beautiful)   She bought a gold bracelet in Athens because she thinks Greek bracelets are

   _____ bracelets in the world.

4. (warm)   She bought a fur hat in Moscow because she thinks Russian hats are

   _____ hats in the world.

5. (modern)   She bought some furniture in Stockholm because she thinks Swedish furniture is

   _____ furniture in the world.

6. (elegant)   She bought an evening gown in Paris because she thinks French evening gowns are

   _____ evening gowns in the world.

7. (pretty)   She bought a Chinese rug in Hong Kong because she thinks Chinese rugs are

   _____ rugs in the world.

8. (good)   She bought a suit in London because she thinks English suits are

   _____ suits in the world.

9. (safe)   She bought a car in Tokyo because she thinks Japanese cars are

   _____ cars in the world.

10. (accurate)   She bought a watch in Geneva because she thinks Swiss watches are

    _____ watches in the world.

11. She also bought . . . . in . . . . because she thinks . . . .

    . . . .

D. WONDERFUL WHAMMO PRODUCTS

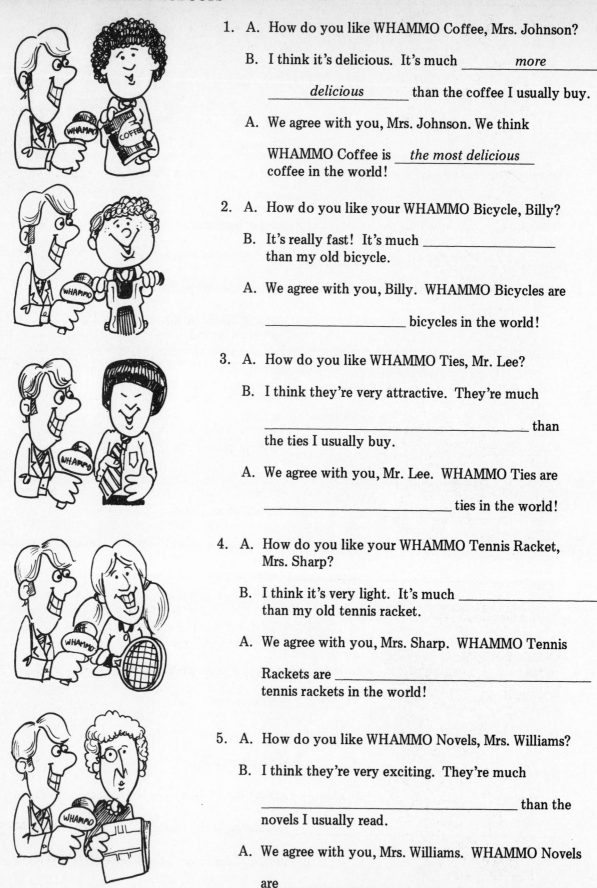

1. A. How do you like WHAMMO Coffee, Mrs. Johnson?

    B. I think it's delicious. It's much _____more_____

    _____delicious_____ than the coffee I usually buy.

    A. We agree with you, Mrs. Johnson. We think

    WHAMMO Coffee is _the most delicious_
    coffee in the world!

2. A. How do you like your WHAMMO Bicycle, Billy?

    B. It's really fast! It's much _____
    than my old bicycle.

    A. We agree with you, Billy. WHAMMO Bicycles are

    _____ bicycles in the world!

3. A. How do you like WHAMMO Ties, Mr. Lee?

    B. I think they're very attractive. They're much

    _____ than
    the ties I usually buy.

    A. We agree with you, Mr. Lee. WHAMMO Ties are

    _____ ties in the world!

4. A. How do you like your WHAMMO Tennis Racket,
    Mrs. Sharp?

    B. I think it's very light. It's much _____
    than my old tennis racket.

    A. We agree with you, Mrs. Sharp. WHAMMO Tennis

    Rackets are _____
    tennis rackets in the world!

5. A. How do you like WHAMMO Novels, Mrs. Williams?

    B. I think they're very exciting. They're much

    _____ than the
    novels I usually read.

    A. We agree with you, Mrs. Williams. WHAMMO Novels

    are _____
    novels in the world!

6. A. How do you like your WHAMMO Fan, Mr. Nathan?

B. I think it's very quiet. It's much _____ than my old fan.

A. We agree with you, Mr. Nathan. WHAMMO Fans are

_____ fans in the world!

7. A. How do you like WHAMMO Shampoo, Mrs. Schultz?

B. I think it's wonderful! Now my hair is soft and shiny.

It's much _____ and _____ than before.

A. We agree with you, Mrs. Schultz. Women who wash

with WHAMMO Shampoo have _____

_____ and _____ hair in the world!

8. A. How do you like WHAMMO Soap, Mrs. Rinaldi?

B. I think it's terrific. My clothes are so clean and

fresh. They're much _____

and _____ than before.

A. We agree with you, Mrs. Rinaldi. People who wash with WHAMMO Soap have

_____ and _____ clothes in the world!

9. A. How do you like this WHAMMO Cake, Mary?

B. I think it's good. It's much _____ than the cakes I usually eat.

A. We agree with you, Mary. WHAMMO Cakes are

_____ cakes in the world!

10. A. How do you like your WHAMMO Wig, Mrs. Harris?

B. I think it's beautiful. It's much _____

_____ than my old wig.

A. We agree with you, Mrs. Harris. WHAMMO Wigs are

_____ wigs in the world!

E. LOUD AND CLEAR

Fill in the words; then read the sentences aloud.

favorite	ironing	Robert	shirt

brother	German	our	write

1. _____*Robert*_____ is _____*ironing*_____

his _____*favorite*_____ _____*shirt.*_____

2. _____ little _____

can read and _____ _____.

better	recipe	rice	right

are	arrive	morning	mother
	Rome		

3. You're _____! Barbara's

_____ for _____ is

_____ than mine.

4. My _____ and father _____

going to _____ from _____

next Thursday _____.

attractive	birthday	her
racket	received	thirtieth

broken	Friday	Mr.	radiator
Roberts	their	very	were

5. Sara _____ an

_____ tennis

_____ for _____

_____ _____.

6. _____ and Mrs. _____

_____ _____ cold last

_____ because _____

_____ was

_____.

46

A. Complete the sentences.

Ex. Will you be back soon?

Yes, _____*I will.*_____ _____*I'll*_____
be back in fifteen minutes.

Ex. Will George be home soon?

No, _____*he won't.*_____ He's
busy tonight.

1. Will the movie begin soon?

Yes, _____. _____
begin in a few minutes.

2. Will Aunt Helen get out of the hospital
soon?

No, _____. She's very
sick.

3. Will you be ready soon?

Yes, _____. _____
be ready in a little while.

4. Will the boss be in the office tomorrow?

No, _____. He's on
vacation.

5. Will your friends be here soon?

Yes, _____. _____
be here in half an hour.

B. Complete the sentences with **might** or
should.

| might   should |

1. I don't think I'll go swimming with you. I'm

afraid I _____ drown.

2. What do you think? _____ I
buy a bicycle or a motorcycle?

3. I _____ get married next

month, or I _____ get married
next year. I really can't decide.

4. John's doctor thinks he _____
drink milk because it's good for him.

C. Fill in the blanks.

Ex. A. Are these Betty's glasses?

B. No, they aren't _____*hers.*_____

1. A. Is that Fred's English book?

B. No, it isn't _____.

2. A. Is this your car?

B. No, it isn't _____.

3. A. Is that Mr. and Mrs. Wong's house?

B. No, it isn't _____.

4. A. Are these my gloves?

B. No, they aren't _____.

D. Fill in the blanks.

Ex. Dan is _____*nicer than*_____ Bill.
　　　　　　　　nice

1. Michael is _____ John.
　　　　　　　　　　tall

2. Carol is _____ Judy.
　　　　　　　　　capable

3. My dog is _____
　　　　　　　　friendly
your dog.

4. Joe's bicycle is _____
　　　　　　　　　　fast
Tim's bicycle.

5. Patty's cake is _____
　　　　　　　　　　delicious

_____ my cake.

E. Complete the sentences.

Ex. John (rich) _____isn't as_____

_____rich as_____ Carl, but he's

much (happy) _____happier._____

1. Henry's neighborhood (interesting)

_____

Jack's neighborhood, but it's much

(safe) _____ .

2. Elizabeth (nice) _____

_____ Katherine, but she's

much (talented) _____ .

3. Doris (young) _____

_____ Jane, but she's

much (healthy) _____ .

4. My apartment (elegant) _____

_____ your

apartment, but it's much (big)

_____ .

5. Tom's car (new) _____
Lee's car, but it's much (good)

_____ .

F. Fill in the blanks.

Ex. Harry is _____the kindest_____ person I
know.   kind

1. Mary is _____ person I
know.   nice

2. Uncle Herbert is _____

_____ person in
            intelligent
our family.

3. Bill has _____ apartment
            large
in the neighborhood.

4. Mrs. Blake is _____
                        interesting
teacher in our school.

5. Jack is _____ person
           honest
I know.

G. LISTEN

Listen and put a circle around the correct
answer.

Ex. Alice	(Yes) / No	Margaret
1. Bob	Yes / No	Bill
2.	Yes / No	
3. Herman	Yes / No	David
4. Madrid 100°F/38°C	Yes / No	Stockholm 32°F/0°C
5. Jack	Yes / No	Carl

48

A. HOW DO I GET THERE?

MILK ST.

butcher shop	high school
clinic	barber shop
drug store	post office
bakery	shoe store
bank	super-market
laundromat	police station

across from	on the right	walk down
between	on the left	walk up
next to		

24

1. A. Excuse me. Would you please tell me how to get to the barber shop from here?

   B. _____*Walk up*_____ Milk Street and you'll see the barber shop __*on*__ _____*the right*_____, across from the _____*clinic*_____.

2. A. Excuse me. Would you please tell me how to get to the high school from here?

   B. _____ Milk Street and you'll see the high school _____, across from the _____.

3. A. Excuse me. Would you please tell me how to get to the butcher shop from here?

   B. _____ Milk Street and you'll see the butcher shop _____, next to the _____.

4. A. Excuse me. Would you please tell me how to get to the supermarket from here?

   B. _____ Milk Street and you'll see the supermarket _____, _____ the shoe store and the police station.

5. A. Excuse me. Would you please tell me how to get to the clinic from here?

   B. _____ Milk Street and you'll see the clinic _____, _____ the barber shop.

49

B. **WHICH WAY?**

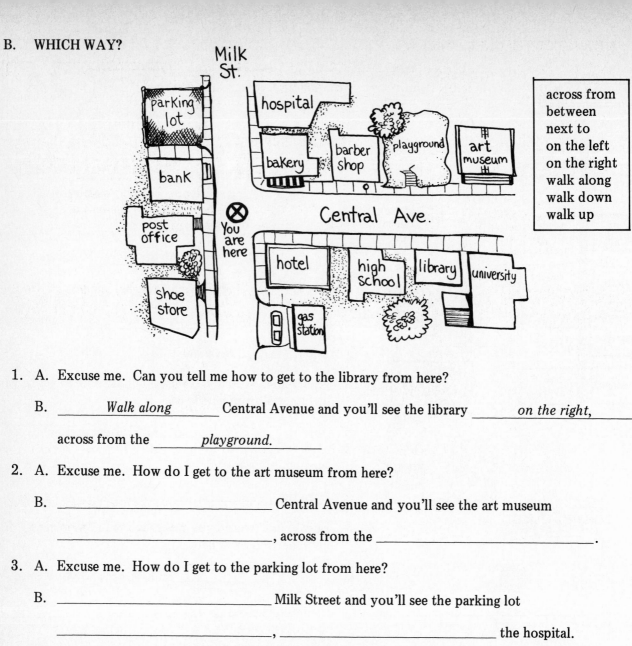

1. A. Excuse me. Can you tell me how to get to the library from here?

    B. _____*Walk along*_____ Central Avenue and you'll see the library _____*on the right,*_____
    across from the _____*playground.*_____

2. A. Excuse me. How do I get to the art museum from here?

    B. _____ Central Avenue and you'll see the art museum
    _____, across from the _____.

3. A. Excuse me. How do I get to the parking lot from here?

    B. _____ Milk Street and you'll see the parking lot
    _____, _____ the hospital.

4. A. Excuse me. Can you tell me how to get to the shoe store from here?

    B. _____ Milk Street and you'll see the shoe store
    _____, _____ the post office.

5. A. Excuse me. How do I get to the university from here?

    B. _____ Central Avenue and you'll see the university
    _____, next to the _____.

6. A. Excuse me. Can you tell me how to get to the playground from here?

    B. _____ Central Avenue and you'll see the playground
    _____, _____ the
    _____ and the _____.

50

C. MRS. BROWN NEEDS YOUR HELP

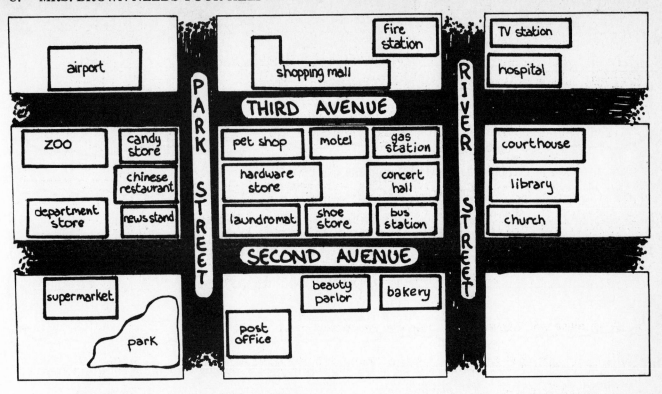

Mrs. Brown is very busy today. She has to go to many stores, but she doesn't know the city very well. She needs YOUR help.

1. She's at the post office, and she's going to the bakery because she wants to buy fresh bread. Tell her how to get there.

_____*Walk up*_____ Park Street to Second Avenue and _____*turn right.*_____

_____*Walk along*_____ Second Avenue and you'll see the bakery

____*on the right*____ , ____*across from*____ the bus station.

2. She's at the bakery, and she wants to go to the hardware store because she has to fix her sink.

_____ Second Avenue to Park Street and _____

_____. _____ Park Street and you'll see the hardware

store _____, _____ the pet shop and the laundromat.

3. She's at the hardware store, and she's going to the shopping mall because she needs a raincoat.

_____ Park Street to Third Avenue and _____.

_____ Third Avenue and you'll see the shopping mall

_____, _____ the motel.

4. She's at the shopping mall, and she's very hungry. She wants to go to the Chinese restaurant for lunch.

_____ Third Avenue to Park Street and _____ .

_____ Park Street and you'll see the Chinese restaurant

_____ , _____ the candy store.

5. Mrs. Brown is at the Chinese restaurant, and she wants to go to the library to get a book.

_____ Park Street to Second Avenue and _____ .

_____ Second Avenue to River Street and _____ .

_____ River Street and you'll see the library _____

_____ , _____ the _____ and the _____ .

6. She's at the library, and she wants to go to the shoe store. She's looking for a more comfortable pair of shoes.

. . . .

. . . .

. . . .

7. She's at the shoe store, and now she has to visit a friend in the hospital.

. . . .

. . . .

. . . .

8. Mrs. Brown is very tired, and she wants to sit in the park and rest before she goes home.

. . . .

. . . .

. . . .

Thank you for your help.

D. IN A HURRY

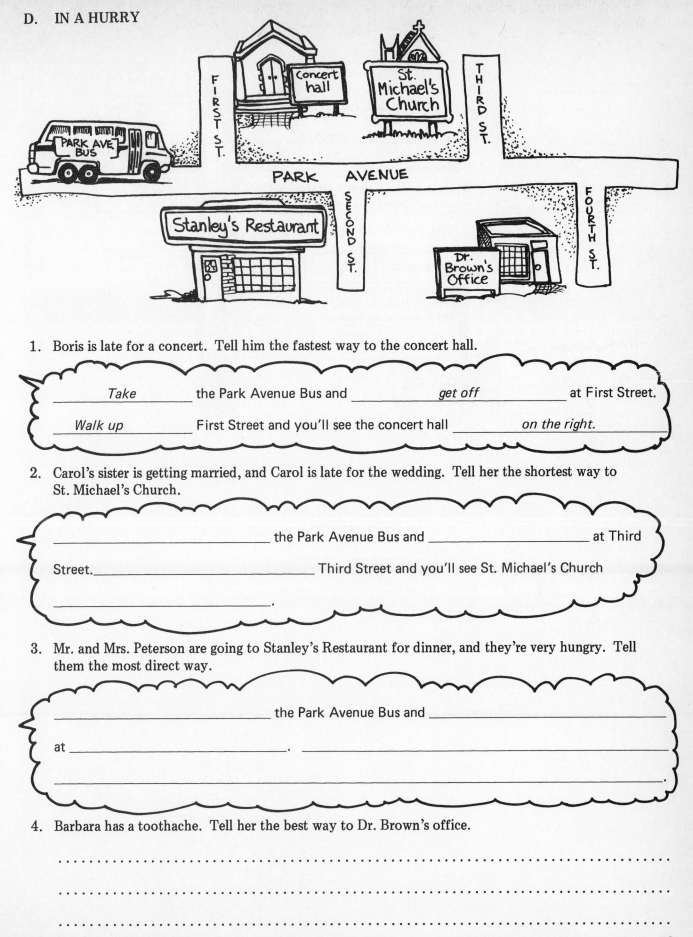

1. Boris is late for a concert. Tell him the fastest way to the concert hall.

_____*Take*_____ the Park Avenue Bus and _____*get off*_____ at First Street.

_____*Walk up*_____ First Street and you'll see the concert hall _____*on the right.*_____

2. Carol's sister is getting married, and Carol is late for the wedding. Tell her the shortest way to St. Michael's Church.

_____ the Park Avenue Bus and _____ at Third Street._____ Third Street and you'll see St. Michael's Church

_____ .

3. Mr. and Mrs. Peterson are going to Stanley's Restaurant for dinner, and they're very hungry. Tell them the most direct way.

_____ the Park Avenue Bus and _____

at _____ . _____

_____ .

4. Barbara has a toothache. Tell her the best way to Dr. Brown's office.

. . . .

. . . .

. . . .

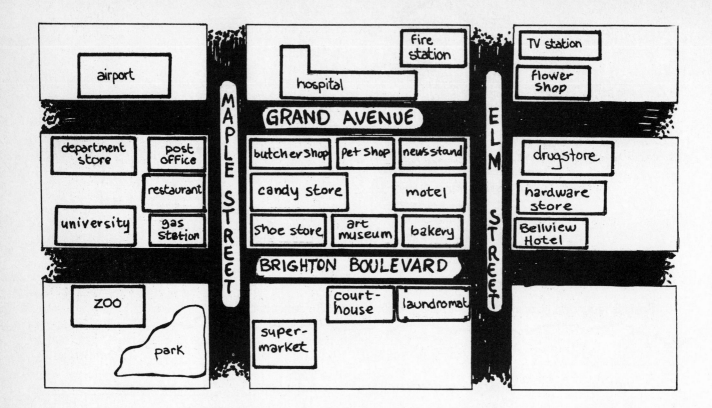

Listen and fill in the correct places.

1. He went to the _____.

2. She went to the _____.

3. They went to the _____.

4. He went to the _____.

5. She went to the _____.

6. They went to the _____.

7. They went to the _____.

A. WHAT DO YOU THINK?

25

1. A. I think Gloria is a terrible tennis player. What do you think?

   B. I agree. She plays tennis _____*terribly.*_____

2. A. Is Arthur a graceful dancer?

   B. Yes. He dances very _____.

3. A. I think Frank is a careless driver.

   B. He certainly is. He drives very _____.

4. A. Is Rita a slow worker?

   B. Yes. She works very _____.

5. A. Is Natasha an accurate translator?

   B. She certainly is. She translates everything very _____.

6. A. I think Charlie is a very sloppy eater.

   B. I agree. He eats very _____.

7. A. Is Susan a fast swimmer?

   B. Yes, she is. She swims very _____.

8. A. Is your mother a good baker?

   B. She certainly is. She bakes very _____.

9. A. I think Shirley is a _____ skater. What do you think?

   B. I agree. She skates beautifully.

10. A. I think Mr. Green is a _____ worker.

    B. I think so, too. He works very patiently.

11. A. Is George a _____ football player?

    B. Yes. He plays football very well.

12. A. Is Gladys a hard worker?

    B. Yes. She works very _____.

B. ANSWER

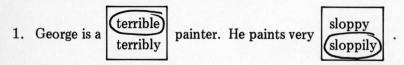

CAREFUL
(CAREFULLY)

Put a circle around the correct word.

1. George is a (terrible) / terribly painter. He paints very sloppy / (sloppily) .

2. I don't like to play cards with Harry. He plays very dishonest / dishonestly .

3. Richard is a slow / slowly chess player, but he plays very good / well .

4. Frieda is very graceful / gracefully . She dances beautiful / beautifully .

5. According to Mario, you can live cheap / cheaply in Rome.

6. Michael plays tennis terrible / terribly , but he's a good / well baseball player.

7. Anna plays the violin very bad / badly , but her family listens patient / patiently .

8. I usually drive careful / carefully , but I was very careless / carelessly yesterday.

C. LISTEN

Listen and put a circle around the correct answer.

1.	neat / neatly	4.	beautiful / beautifully	7.	sloppy / sloppily	10.	slow / slowly
2.	sloppy / sloppily	5.	graceful / gracefully	8.	elegant / elegantly	11.	careful / carefully
3.	accurate / accurately	6.	bad / badly	9.	safe / safely	12.	easy / easily

56

D. THE BOSS IS ANGRY

Fill in the correct words.

early	_earlier_	neat(ly)	⎰ _____ ⎱
careful	_more carefully_		⎱ _____ ⎰
late	_____	politely	_____
loud(ly)	⎰ _____ ⎱	slowly	⎰ _____ ⎱
	⎱ _____ ⎰		⎱ _____ ⎰

1. A. Mr. Smith, I think you dress too sloppily.

   B. You're right, Mr. Sharp. I'll try to dress ⎰ _neater._ ⎱
      ⎱ _more neatly._ ⎰

2. A. I also think you speak too softly.

   B. You're right, Mr. Sharp. I'll try to speak _____.

3. A. And, Mr. Smith, I think you get to the office too late.

   B. You're right, Mr. Sharp. I'll try to get to the office _____.

4. A. And I'm upset, Mr. Smith, because you type too carelessly.

   B. You're right, Mr. Sharp. I'll try to type _____.

5. A. Also, Mr. Smith, everybody says you speak too quickly.

   B. You're right, Mr. Sharp. I'll try to speak _____.

6. A. And before you leave, Mr. Smith, I want to tell you that everybody is upset because you go home too early.

   B. You're right, Mr. Sharp. I'll try to go home _____.

   A. That's all, Mr. Smith. You can go now.

   B. Thank you, Mr. Sharp.

7.   Why did I speak so impolitely to Mr. Smith?

   Next time I'll try to speak _____.

E. WHAT'S THE WORD?

Put a circle around the correct words.

1. If (I move) / I'll move to Boston, I live / (I'll live) on Main Street.

2. If you call / you'll call your mother, she'll be very happy.

3. If the mechanic fixes our car on time, we drive / we'll drive to Centerville.

4. If it rains / it'll rain today, we won't go to the park.

5. If I'm not in a hurry tonight, I write / I'll write to her.

6. If she isn't / won't be sick, she'll go to school.

7. If they're / they'll be tired tomorrow, they don't go / won't go to work.

8. If John doesn't buy a car, he buys / he'll buy a motorcycle.

F. IF

1. If we __go__ to London, __we'll__ visit our cousin.

2. If they _____ their homework tonight, their teacher _____ happy.

3. If the weather _____ good, George _____ swimming this weekend.

4. If he _____ swimming this weekend, _____ a wonderful time.

5. If you don't eat your dinner tonight, _____ hungry.

6. If _____ tired, they'll go to sleep early tonight.

7. If it _____, she'll wear her new raincoat.

8. If you _____ too many cookies after dinner tonight, _____ get a stomachache.

9. If I _____ too much champagne at my sister's wedding, _____ get a headache.

10. If we _____ a boy, _____ him Peter.

58

G. SCRAMBLED SENTENCES

Unscramble the sentences.

1. if   she   she'll   misses   bus   the   walk

   ___*If she misses the bus*___ , ___*she'll walk.*___

2. if   he   he'll   concert   goes   his   suit,   the   to   wear

   _____ , _____ .

3. if   she   she'll   cook   isn't   dinner   tired

   _____ , _____ .

4. if   I'm   I'll   busy   not   you   visit

   _____ , _____ .

5. if   you   you'll   be   don't   school   finish   sorry

   _____ , _____ .

6. if   he   he'll   a   get   good   hard   job   works

   _____ , _____ .

H. YOU DECIDE

Complete the sentences with any vocabulary you wish.

1. If the weather is bad tomorrow, ...

2. If we hitchhike to work, ...

3. If I don't sleep well tonight, ...

4. If you don't fix the broken window, ...

5. If he doesn't cut his hair, ...

6. If . . . . , they'll go to a restaurant tonight.

7. If . . . . , his mother will be happy.

8. If . . . ., his mother will be sad.

9. If . . . ., her boss will fire her.

10. If . . . ., their friends will be jealous.

59

I. YOU DECIDE: *WHAT MIGHT HAPPEN?*

1. Margaret shouldn't sing so loud.

    If she sings too loud, she might . . . .

2. Paul shouldn't eat so much.

    If he eats too much, he might . . . .

3. Your friends shouldn't do their homework so quickly.

    If they do their homework too quickly, they might . . . .

4. Richard shouldn't worry so much.

    If he worries too much, he might . . . .

5. You shouldn't ski so carelessly.

    If. . . . .

6. Your husband shouldn't speak so impolitely to his boss.

    If . . . .

7. Your children shouldn't go to bed so late.

    If . . . .

8. Bill shouldn't play his rock and roll records so loud.

    If . . . .

9. Betty shouldn't play cards so dishonestly.

    If . . . .

10. You shouldn't talk so much.

    If . . . .

J. **PLEASE DON'T!**

1. Please don't bake an apple pie for dessert!

   Why not?

   If you bake an apple pie for dessert, I'll eat too much.

   If _____ *I eat* _____ too much, __*I'll*__ get fat.

   And if _____ fat, _____ have to buy new clothes.

   So please don't bake an apple pie for dessert!

2. Please don't play your loud rock and roll records all day!

   Why not?

   If you play your records all day, the neighbors will be upset.

   If _____ upset, _____ tell the landlord.

   And if _____ the landlord, _____ get angry.

   So please don't play your loud rock and roll records all day!

3. Please don't buy Tommy a science fiction book!

   Why not?

   If you buy him a science fiction book, he'll read all night.

   If _____ all night, _____ be tired in the morning.

   If _____ tired in the morning, he won't get up on time.

   If _____ get up on time, _____ be late for school.

   And if _____ late for school, _____ miss his English test.

   So please don't buy Tommy a science fiction book!

A. Complete the sentences.

Ex. He's a careless driver.

He drives very _____carelessly._____

1. She's a graceful dancer.

She dances very _____.

2. He's a terrible soccer player.

He plays soccer _____.

3. They're sloppy eaters.

They eat very _____.

4. We're hard workers.

We work very _____.

B. Put a circle around the correct answer.

1. She's not a | good |
                | well | tennis player.

She plays tennis | bad |
                 | badly | .

2. Mary types | quick |
              | quickly | , but she isn't

| accurate |
| accurately | .

3. I don't dress | beautiful |
                 | beautifully | , but I

dress | neat |
      | neatly | .

4. John usually drives | safe |
                       | safely | , but

yesterday he was | careless |
                 | carelessly | .

C. Complete the sentences.

Ex. Edward dresses too sloppily.

He should try to dress ___{ neater. }___
                          { more neatly. }

1. Albert leaves work too early.

He should try to leave work _____.

2. Linda speaks too impolitely.

She should try to speak _____.

3. Alice works too slowly.

She should try to work _____.

4. Peter talks too softly.

He should try to talk _____.

D. Complete the sentences.

Ex. If they ___have___ a girl, ___they'll___ name her Jane.

1. If the weather _____ good, we'll go sailing on Saturday.

2. If you _____ all these cigarettes, _____ get a headache.

3. If _____ hungry tonight, I'll eat a big dinner.

4. If Tommy _____ his homework tonight, his teacher _____ happy.

E. Put a circle around the correct answer.

1. If | we go |
      | we'll go | to the supermarket this

afternoon, | we buy |
           | we'll buy | some bread.

2. If it $\boxed{\begin{array}{c}\text{won't}\\\text{doesn't}\end{array}}$ rain tomorrow, $\boxed{\begin{array}{c}\text{she'll go}\\\text{she goes}\end{array}}$

swimming.

3. If I eat too much tonight, I $\boxed{\begin{array}{c}\text{get}\\\text{might get}\end{array}}$

a stomachache.

4. If my parents $\boxed{\begin{array}{c}\text{will feel}\\\text{feel}\end{array}}$ better tonight,

they $\boxed{\begin{array}{c}\text{visit}\\\text{might visit}\end{array}}$ our neighbors.

F.   LISTEN

Listen and fill in the correct places.

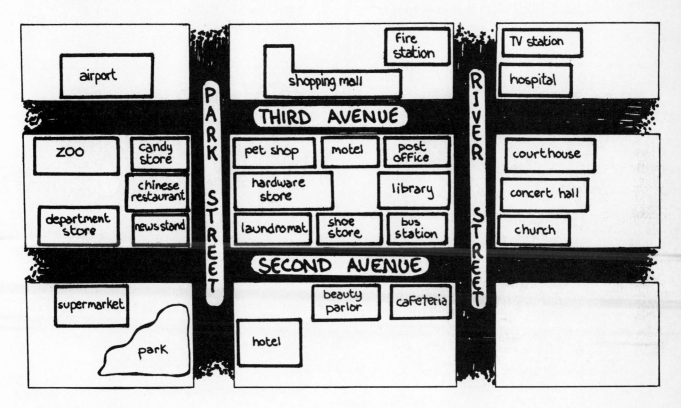

1. She went to the _____.

2. He went to the _____.

3. They went to the _____.

4. She went to the _____.

5. They went to the _____.

A. BAD WEATHER

have a picnic	ride her bicycle	wait for the bus
plant flowers	swim	wash her car
play baseball	take a walk	

Yesterday morning it was sunny and beautiful, but at 1:00 in the afternoon it started to rain.

1. What was Janet doing when it started to rain?

2. What was Mr. Williams doing when it started to rain?

She was washing her car.

3. What were you and Mary doing?

4. What was Michael doing?

5. What were your friends doing?

6. What was Nancy doing?

7. What were Mr. and Mrs. Blake doing?

8. What was your brother doing?

9. What were YOU doing?

B. WHAT WERE THEY DOING?

1. They (wait) _____*were waiting*_____ for the bus when it started to snow.

2. She (wash) _____ her hair when her boyfriend called.

3. They (play) _____ cards when their parents got home.

4. I (take) _____ a bath when the plumber arrived.

5. We (leave) _____ the discotheque when we saw our English teacher.

6. She (look for) _____ her pocketbook when the lights went out.

7. My children (make) _____ breakfast when we got up.

8. He (talk) _____ to his friend when the teacher asked him a difficult question.

C. WHAT'S THE WORD?

Put a circle around the correct word.

1. When I saw John, he was getting
   | on |
   | off |
   | into |
   a taxi.

2. George was walking
   | out of |
   | off |
   | of |
   the library when he saw his brother.

3. Anna got
   | from |
   | off |
   | up |
   the bus and walked home.

4. We walked
   | into |
   | out of |
   | in |
   the nearest restaurant because we were hungry.

5. Get
   | at |
   | up |
   | on |
   the subway at First Avenue.

6. Helen was riding her bicycle
   | through |
   | along |
   | in |
   Main Street.

7. I'm going to get
   | out of |
   | off |
   | into |
   the car because I'm feeling carsick.

D. TOO EARLY

Jim was embarrassed when he arrived at his girlfriend Mary's house for dinner last night. He got there MUCH too early, and Mary and her family weren't ready.

1. What was Mary doing when Jim arrived?

   She was cleaning the living room.

3. What was Mary's father doing?

   _____

5. What was her older sister Betty doing?

   _____

2. What was Mary's mother doing?

   _____

4. What were her little brother and sister doing?

   _____

6. What was her brother Paul doing?

   _____

E. NOBODY WANTS TO

myself	yourself	himself	herself	ourselves	yourselves	themselves

1. Nobody wants to go to the movies with me.

   I'll have to go to the movies by _____*myself.*_____

2. Nobody wants to go to the baseball game with her.

   She'll have to go to the baseball game by _____.

3. Nobody wants to go bowling with us.

   We'll have to go bowling by _____.

4. Nobody wants to take a walk with you.

   You'll have to take a walk by _____.

5. Nobody wants to drive to the airport with them.

   They'll have to drive to the airport by _____.

6. Nobody wants to have dinner with him.

   He'll have to have dinner by _____.

7. Nobody wants to play cards with you and your brother.

   You'll have to play cards by _____.

F. WHAT'S THE WORD?   Put a circle around the correct word.

1. We were standing
   | on |
   | into |
   | over |
   the corner.

2. They were driving
   | out of |
   | over |
   | through |
   a bridge.

3. A can of paint fell
   | to |
   | on |
   | along |
   me.

4. Natasha always walks
   | to |
   | under |
   | along |
   work.

5. She was riding
   | in |
   | along |
   | through |
   an elevator.

6. Arthur likes to look
   | to |
   | on |
   | at |
   himself

   | on |
   | in |
   | at |
   the mirror.

7. Lois is afraid because she walked

   | through |
   | over |
   | under |
   a ladder.

8. Our children can cook breakfast

   | to |
   | at |
   | by |
   themselves.

67

G.   WHAT HAPPENED?

bake	dance	shave	study
burn	have	skate	walk
cut	ride	sleep	

1. Alice hurt herself while _____ *she was* _____

_____ *skating.* _____

3. Sally saw a friend while _____

_____ her bicycle along Park Street.

5. Bob stepped on Jane's feet while _____

_____ together.

7. Mr. and Mrs. Brown _____ themselves while _____

_____ cookies.

2. I met my neighbor while _____

_____ home from work.

4. Peter fell asleep while_____

_____ .

6. I _____ myself while _____

_____ .

8. Tommy _____ a nightmare while

_____

at a friend's house.

68

H. LOUD AND CLEAR

Fill in the words; then read the sentences aloud.

eat	pieces	pizza	Rita	three

1. ____*Rita*____ is going to ____*eat*____

____*three*____ ____*pieces*____

of ____*pizza.*____

delicious	didn't	dinner	finish
	it	this	

2. _____ _____ was

_____ , but we

_____ _____ _____ ____ .

Green	police	stealing	Street
	thief		

3. Call the _____ ! A _____

is _____ a car on

_____ _____ !

busy	children	Ginger	is	office
	Smith	with		

4. _____ _____ sitting in

Doctor Smith's _____ _____

her sick _____ . Doctor

_____ is _____ .

between	fifteen	leave	Rio
	three		

5. The plane to _____ is going to

_____ _____ three and

_____ _____ .

big	building	city	in	is
	live	sister		

6. My _____ Hilda _____ going to

_____ _____ an apartment

_____ in a

_____ _____ .

69

A. WHAT'S THE WORD?

could	can
couldn't	can't

1. When I first arrived in this country, I was embarrassed because I _____couldn't_____ speak English.

   Now I'm happy because I _can_ speak English very well.

2. _____ Betty read when she was three years old?

   Yes, she _____. She was very bright.

3. We _____ finish our dinner last night because we were too full.

4. My brother is very talented. He _____ speak three languages.

5. Lois _____ buy anything at the store because she didn't have any money.

6. When I was young, I _____ go dancing every night. I was very energetic.

7. Shirley is jealous because her younger sister _____ sing beautifully, and she

   _____.

8. _____ Stuart go to school yesterday?

   No, he _____. He was too sick.

9. Mary _____ play on the basketball team when she was young because she was too short.

   But she wasn't upset because she _____ play on the baseball team.

10. Peter is a terrible dancer, but his little brother _____ dance very well.

11. George was very upset because he _____ go to the discotheque last night.

12. I'm glad you _____ go to the movies with us yesterday.

13. I really want to fire Larry, but I _____. His father is president of the company.

B. YOU DECIDE: *WHY WEREN'T THEY ABLE TO?*

wasn't able to
weren't able to

1. Anita _____*wasn't able to*_____ lift the package because .... *it was too heavy (or)* .....

   .... *she was too weak (or) she was too tired.* ....

2. Tom and Harry _____ do their homework because . . . .

. . . .

3. My brother _____ fall asleep last night because . . . .

. . . .

4. Our cousins _____ go sailing yesterday because . . . .

. . . .

5. Sally _____ wear her mother's shoes because . . . .

. . . .

6. I _____ sit down on the train this morning because . . . .

. . . .

7. My friends _____ eat any onion pizza last night because . . . .

. . . .

8. Maria _____ drive a car last year because . . . .

. . . .

9. We _____ walk home from the party last night because . . . .

. . . .

10. Mr. and Mrs. Blake _____ buy the sofa they wanted because . . . .

. . . .

11. John _____ get into my sports car last Friday because . . . .

. . . .

C.   WHEN THEY WERE YOUNG

{ could { was/were able to {		{ couldn't { wasn't/weren't able to {		had to

1. When I was young, I was angry because I _____ { *couldn't*
{ *wasn't able to* { _____ play with my friends after school.

    I _____ *had to* _____ get home early and take care of my little brother and sister.

2. When Janet was young, she wanted to watch TV after school every day, but she _____

    because she _____ do her homework.

3. Richard's teachers always gave him a lot of homework, and his parents _____
    help him because they were too busy.

4. Margaret's brother _____ go with her when she went out on dates because, in
    her mother's opinion, she was too young to go out by herself.

5. Nancy was jealous because her older brothers _____ go to bed late, but she

    _____ . She _____ go to bed at 7:00 every evening.

6. When William was thirteen years old, his father got a job in Boston and the family moved there.

    William was sad because he _____ see his old friends very often.

7. Roger was jealous of his rich friends because they _____ eat at fancy restaurants

    and they _____ buy expensive clothes. He was embarrassed because he

    _____ wear his brother's old clothes.

8. Andrew was upset because he wanted to have long hair, but he _____ . He

    _____ go to the barber every month because his parents liked short hair.

D. YOU DECIDE: *WHY DIDN'T THEY ENJOY THEMSELVES?*

myself   yourself   himself   herself   ourselves   yourselves   themselves
{ couldn't
{ wasn't/weren't able to }

1. I didn't enjoy _____*myself*_____ at the beach yesterday. It was very windy, and I

.......................*couldn't go swimming (or) wasn't able to go sailing.*..........................

2. Bobby and his friends didn't enjoy _____ in the park yesterday. It was raining,

and they ....

3. Susan didn't enjoy _____ at the restaurant yesterday. She was very nervous

about her examination, and she ....

4. George didn't enjoy _____ at the movies last night. It was very crowded and

noisy, and he ....

5. I didn't enjoy _____ at Gloria's party last Friday. There were too many people

there, and I ....

6. We didn't enjoy _____ on our vacation last winter. We got sick, and we

....

E. THEY'LL BE ABLE TO

couldn't   will be able to

1. Martha _____*couldn't*_____ find her shoes in the yard last night, but I'm sure _____*she'll be*_____

_____*able to*_____ find them this morning.

2. We _____ move to our new apartment last month. I hope _____

_____ move there next month.

3. I _____ help Linda take care of her baby last week, but I think _____

_____ help her this week.

4. Harry and Steve _____ go bowling with us last Friday, but I think _____

_____ go bowling with us next week.

5. Roger _____ finish his homework last night, but I know _____

_____ finish it tonight.

F.   CARMEN

will/won't be able to

Carmen is a very energetic person.

1. She goes jogging every morning.
2. She rides her bicycle to school every day.
3. She plays soccer on the school team.
4. She swims every afternoon.
5. She does exercises every evening.

She's also very talented and capable.

6. She plays the guitar.
7. She writes her own songs.
8. She bakes delicious cakes and pies.
9. She makes her own clothes.

Last week Carmen went skiing, and unfortunately she broke her leg. The doctor says she'll have to rest her leg all month. Carmen is upset because:

1. _____ *She won't be able to go jogging every morning.* _____

2. _____

3. _____

4. _____

5. _____

Fortunately there are many things Carmen WILL be able to do.

6. _____ *She'll be able to play the guitar.* _____

7. _____

8. _____

9. _____

G. I'M SORRY

> won't be able to   have/has got to

1. I'm really sorry. My husband and I _____*won't be able to*_____ go to the tennis match with you tomorrow. _____*We've got to*_____ take our son to the doctor.

2. I'm terribly sorry. My daughter _____ go to her ballet lesson this afternoon. _____ take care of her little brother.

3. I'm sorry. My children _____ go to the baseball game with you on Saturday. _____ study for an examination.

4. I'm really upset. My father _____ drive us to the beach tomorrow because _____ take my sister to the dentist.

5. I feel terrible. My wife and I _____ help you paint your apartment on Sunday. _____ visit our cousin in the hospital.

H. LISTEN

Listen to each story twice and then answer the questions you hear.

Mr. and Mrs. Smith's Vacation

1. a. they were too busy.
   b. they were too old.
   c. the ocean was too cold.

2. a. better than today.
   b. worse than today.
   c. very cold.

3. a. they're too disappointed.
   b. they've got to leave early in the morning.
   c. the ocean will be cold.

Helen's English Examination

4. a. English homework.
   b. briefcase.
   c. glasses.

5. a. This morning.
   b. Last night.
   c. After the examination.

6. a. she got to school late.
   b. she did very well on her English examination.
   c. she didn't do well on her English examination.

75

A. Complete the sentences.

Ex. She (wash) _____*was washing*_____ her hair
when her boyfriend called.

1. We (paint) _____ the house
when it started to rain.

2. I (drive) _____ to work
when I got a flat tire.

3. They (study) _____
English when the lights went out.

4. Mary fell down while she (skate) _____

_____.

5. John saw an accident while he (ride) _____

_____ his bicycle.

6. We met our neighbor while we (walk) _____

_____ home from work.

7. I cut myself while I (make) _____

_____ lunch.

B. Fill in the blanks.

Ex. I enjoyed _____*myself*_____ at the concert.

1. We didn't enjoy _____ at the
movies.

2. My father cut _____ while he
was shaving.

3. Did you and your wife enjoy

_____ at Robert's party?

4. Mr. and Mrs. Brown burned

_____ while they were
baking cookies.

5. Nobody went to the baseball game with
Judy. She had to go to the baseball game

by _____.

6. Did you fix the TV by _____
or did your husband help you?

C. Put a circle around the correct word.

1. When I saw Tom, he was getting
$\boxed{\begin{array}{c} \text{on} \\ \text{off} \\ \text{into} \end{array}}$

a taxi.

2. I usually get
$\boxed{\begin{array}{c} \text{at} \\ \text{up} \\ \text{off} \end{array}}$ the bus at Third Street.

3. When our teacher walked
$\boxed{\begin{array}{c} \text{out of} \\ \text{off} \\ \text{of} \end{array}}$ the

room, everybody started to talk.

4. We walked
$\boxed{\begin{array}{c} \text{in} \\ \text{into} \\ \text{out of} \end{array}}$ the nearest building

because it was raining.

5. Why were you getting
$\boxed{\begin{array}{c} \text{out of} \\ \text{off} \\ \text{from} \end{array}}$ a police car

at 8:00 this morning?

6. We
$\boxed{\begin{array}{c} \text{could} \\ \text{couldn't} \\ \text{can't} \end{array}}$ finish our dinner last night

because we were too full.

7. I'm sorry you
$\boxed{\begin{array}{c} \text{couldn't} \\ \text{can't} \\ \text{won't be able to} \end{array}}$ go to the

theater with us yesterday.

8. When Peter was young, he wanted to talk on
the telephone all afternoon, but he

$\boxed{\begin{array}{c} \text{could} \\ \text{couldn't} \\ \text{had to} \end{array}}$ because he $\boxed{\begin{array}{c} \text{could} \\ \text{couldn't} \\ \text{had to} \end{array}}$ do his

homework after school.

D. Fill in the blanks.

1. Bill _____ able to go to the beach yesterday because it was raining.

2. I'm glad you _____ able to go to the symphony with us last night.

3. Harry and Steve _____ able to walk home from the party last night because it was too dark.

4. I couldn't move to my new apartment last month, but I think _____ able to move there next month.

5. I feel terrible. I _____

   _____ able to go to your party tomorrow. _____ got to take my son to the doctor.

6. If you want to be the best violinist in your city, _____ got to practice.

7. I'm sorry. My daughter _____ able to go to her violin lesson next Monday.

   _____ got to study for an examination.

E. LISTEN

Listen to the story twice, and then answer the questions you hear.

Poor Bill!

1. a. happy.
   b. upset.
   c. generous.

2. a. got sick.
   b. saw an accident.
   c. got a flat tire.

3. a. his wife.
   b. the airport.
   c. a mechanic.

4. a. early.
   b. late.
   c. on time.

5. a. plane.
   b. train.
   c. bus.

A. GEORGE IS WORRIED ABOUT HIS HEALTH

less	fewer	more

George is worried about his health. He always feels tired, and he doesn't know why.

In January he went to see Doctor Johnson. Doctor Johnson thinks George feels tired because he eats too much salt. According to Doctor Johnson, George must eat (−) _____fewer_____ potato chips, (−) _____ cheese, and (−) _____ salty crackers. Also, he must eat (+) _____ fresh vegetables and (+) _____ rice. George tried Doctor Johnson's diet, but it didn't help.

In February George went to see Doctor Green. Doctor Green thinks George feels tired because he's a little too thin. According to Doctor Green, George must eat (−) _____ yogurt, (−) _____ carrots, and (−) _____ celery. Also, he must eat (+) _____ potatoes, (+) _____ spaghetti, and (+) _____ ice cream. George tried Doctor Johnson's diet, but it didn't help.

In March George went to see Doctor Wilson. Doctor Wilson thinks George feels tired because he eats too much spicy food. According to Doctor Wilson, George must eat (−) _____ garlic, (−) _____ onions, and (−) _____ pizza. Also, he must drink (+) _____ milk and (+) _____ water. George tried Doctor Wilson's diet, but it didn't help.

In April George went to see Doctor Peterson. Doctor Peterson thinks George feels tired because he eats too much sugar. According to Doctor Peterson, George must eat (−) _____ cookies, (−) _____ ice cream, and (−) _____ cake. Also, he must eat (+) _____ meat and (+) _____ fish. George tried Doctor Peterson's diet, but it didn't help either.

Now George needs YOUR help. What do YOU think?

In my opinion, George must eat/drink (−) . . . .

. . . .

Also, he must eat/drink (+) . . . .

. . . .

B.   THEY CAN'T WORK HERE

> We didn't hire Miss Jones because she doesn't type accurately or speak Spanish.

Mr. Smith

1. If you want to work in Mr. Smith's office, you _____ *must type accurately*

_____ *and speak Spanish.*

> We fired Mr. Harris because he doesn't work quickly or dress neatly.

Mrs. Norman

2. If you want to work in Mrs. Norman's office, you _____

_____ .

> We can't hire your cousin because he doesn't speak English or have a car.

Miss Winter

3. If you want to work in Miss Winter's company, you _____

_____ .

> We fired Mrs. Michaels because she isn't patient or kind.

Mrs. Nelson

4. If you want to teach in Mrs. Nelson's school, you _____

_____ .

> We can't hire Fifi because she doesn't act, sing, or dance very well.

Mr. Jackson

5. If you want to act in Mr. Jackson's play, you _____

_____ .

C. TWO VERY DIFFERENT SCHOOLS

Fill in the blanks with the most appropriate words.

> must
> mustn't
> don't have to

Miss Primm's School and The Flower School are very different.

At Miss Primm's you _____must_____ get to school on time every morning. If you're late, your parents _____ write a letter to the teacher.

At The Flower School you _____ get to school on time. If you're a few minutes late, the teachers aren't upset.

At Miss Primm's School the boys _____ wear jackets and ties every day, and the girls _____ wear dresses or skirts. Some girls at Miss Primm's want to wear pants to school, but Miss Primm says they _____.

At The Flower School students can wear any clothes they like, but they _____ dress neatly. The boys are happy because they _____ wear jackets and ties every day, and the girls are happy because they can wear pants.

At Miss Primm's School you _____ have a notebook for every subject, and you _____ forget to take your notebooks to class. Also, at Miss Primm's you _____ be VERY quiet while you're working.

At The Flower School you can talk to your friends, but you _____ talk too loudly.

At Miss Primm's School you _____ stand and say "hello" very politely when a teacher walks into the room.

At The Flower School you _____ stand when a teacher walks into the room. You can sit and work, and nobody thinks you're impolite.

At Miss Primm's School you _____ always agree with your teacher because according to Miss Primm, the teacher is always right.

At The Flower School you _____ agree with your teacher all the time. If you have a different opinion, your teacher will be glad to listen.

D. WRITE ABOUT YOUR SCHOOL

At our school you must . . . .

You mustn't . . . .

You don't have to . . . .

E. YOU DECIDE: *WHAT DID THEY SAY?*

must   mustn't

1. I talked to my doctor and she told me . . . .
. . . . because I'm too heavy.

2. Mary talked to her doctor and he told her . . . .
. . . . because she's too thin.

3. Jack talked to his English teacher and she told him . . . .
. . . . because he makes too many mistakes.

4. I talked to the vet and he told me Rover . . . .
. . . . because he's always sick.

5. Betty talked to the doctor and he told her . . . .
. . . . because she's too nervous.

6. We talked to our landlord and he told us . . . .
. . . . because the neighbors are upset.

analysis	ears	heart	nose	scale	X-ray
blood	examination rooms	hospital gown	nurse	shake	
cardiogram	examine	lead	pressure	stethoscope	
chest	eyes	listen	pulse	take	
doctor	hand	measure	say	weight	

If you go to Dr. Anderson, he'll give you a very complete examination.

1. The _____ will _____ you into one of the _____ _____ .

2. You'll put on a _____ _____ .

3. The _____ will _____ your _____ and _____ "hello."

4. You'll stand on his _____ so he can _____ your height and your _____ .

5. He'll take your _____ .

6. Then he'll _____ your blood _____ .

7. After that, he'll take some _____ for a blood _____ .

8. He'll _____ your _____ , _____ , _____ , and throat.

9. He'll _____ to your _____ with a _____ .

10. Then he'll take a _____ _____ and do a _____ .

G. LOUD AND CLEAR

Fill in the words; then read the sentences aloud.

Helen	her	hire

1. Should I _____*hire*_____ _____*Helen*_____
   or _____*her*_____ sister?

hamburger	hungry	who	whole

2. Who's _____? _____
   wants a _____ on
   _____ wheat bread?

Harry	head	hockey	hurt

3. _____ _____ his
   _____ at the _____
   game.

healthy	her	Hilda	husband

4. _____ and _____
   _____ are _____
   and happy.

half	Henry	his	homework
	hopes		

5. _____ _____ he'll
   finish _____ _____
   in an hour and a _____.

happy	Hawaii	hello	here
	Honolulu		

6. _____! We're _____
   you're _____ in _____,
   _____.

83

A. THEY'LL ALL BE BUSY

1. Will Mr. and Mrs. Jones be busy this afternoon?

   _____
   Yes, they will. They'll

   _____
   be painting their kitchen.

2. Will Peggy be busy this morning?

   _____

   _____

3. Will you and your wife be busy today?

   _____

   _____

4. Will George and Martha be busy tomorrow morning?

   _____

   _____

5. Will you be busy this Saturday?

   _____

   _____

6. Will your children be busy after school today?

   _____

   _____

7. Will Miss Smith be busy this morning?

   _____

   _____

8. Will Sally be busy this afternoon?

   _____

   _____

B. ARTHUR TRIES AGAIN

Arthur was upset after he talked to Gloria. He decided to call Louise.

A. Hi, Louise. This is Arthur.
Can I come over and visit this afternoon?

B. No, Arthur. I'm afraid I won't be home

this afternoon. I'll be . . . .

. . . .

A. Can I come over and visit TOMORROW
afternoon?

B. No, Arthur. I'm afraid I won't be home

tomorrow afternoon. I'll be . . . .

. . . .

A. Can I come over and visit this WEEKEND?

B. No, Arthur. I'll be . . . .

. . . .

A. Can I come over and visit next Tuesday?

B. No, Arthur. I'll be . . . .

. . . .

A. How about some time next SUMMER?

B. No, Arthur. I'll be getting married next
summer.

A. Oh, no! Not again!!

C. UNTIL WHEN?

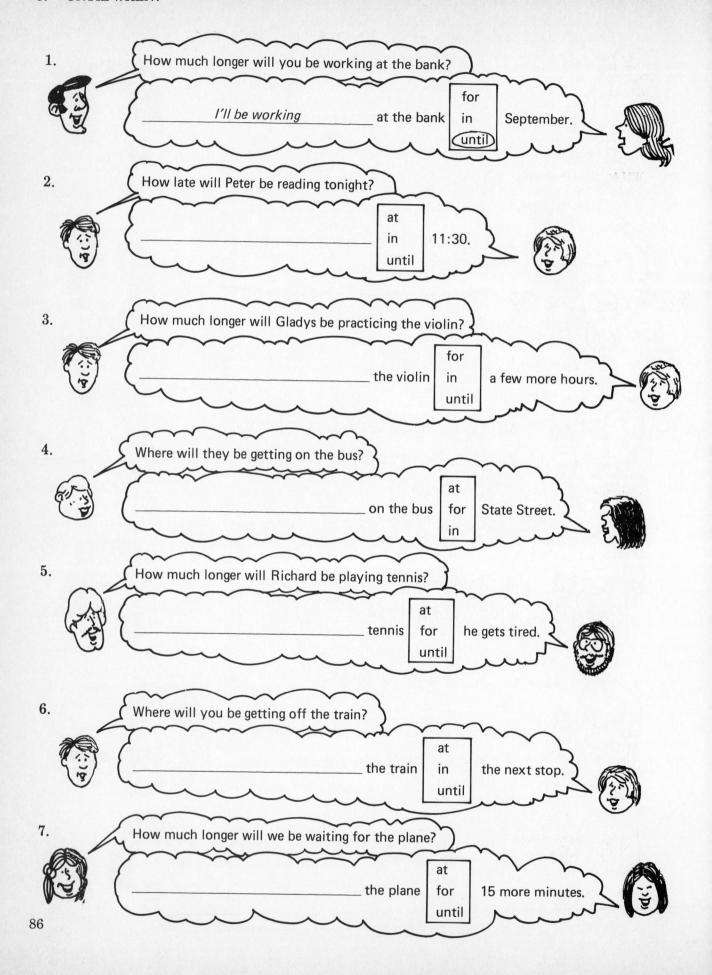

1. How much longer will you be working at the bank?

_____ *I'll be working* _____ at the bank | for / in / **until** | September.

2. How late will Peter be reading tonight?

_____ | at / in / until | 11:30.

3. How much longer will Gladys be practicing the violin?

_____ the violin | for / in / until | a few more hours.

4. Where will they be getting on the bus?

_____ on the bus | at / for / in | State Street.

5. How much longer will Richard be playing tennis?

_____ tennis | at / for / until | he gets tired.

6. Where will you be getting off the train?

_____ the train | at / in / until | the next stop.

7. How much longer will we be waiting for the plane?

_____ the plane | at / for / until | 15 more minutes.

8.

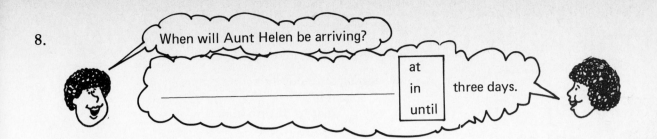

When will Aunt Helen be arriving?

_____ | at / in / until | three days.

D. WHAT'S THE QUESTION?

1. How much longer _____ *will you be taking a bath?* _____

I'll be taking a bath for a few more minutes.

2. A. When _____?

   B. I'll be arriving in Paris at 9 a.m.

3. A. How long _____?

   B. They'll be shopping in the city all afternoon.

4. A. How late _____?

   B. She'll be studying until 10 o'clock.

5. A. How long _____?

   B. He'll be skiing in Europe until March.

6. A. How much longer _____?

   B. I'll be visiting my family for a few more days.

7. A. How long _____?

   B. They'll be working on her car until 5 o'clock.

8. A. How soon _____?

   B. He'll be coming to visit them in two weeks.

9. How much longer _____?

   We'll be sailing for a few more hours.

E.   WHY DON'T YOU . . . . . . ?

1. A. Why don't you call Billy before dinner?

    B. No, I don't want to disturb him. I'm sure _____*he'll be*_____

    _____*practicing the piano.*_____ He always *practices*

    _____*the piano*_____ before dinner.

2. A. Why don't you visit your brother-in-law this morning?

    B. No, I don't want to disturb him. I'm sure _____

    _____. He always _____

    _____ on Saturday morning.

3. A. Why don't you call Sally this evening?

    B. No, I don't want to disturb her. I'm sure _____

    _____. She _____

    _____ every evening.

4. A. Why don't you call William after school?

    B. No, I don't want to disturb him. I'm sure _____

    _____. He_____

    _____ every day after school.

5. A. Why don't you visit Carol and Dan tonight?

    B. No, I don't want to disturb them. I'm sure _____

    _____. They usually _____

    _____ on Thursday night.

6. A. Why don't you call Jane after breakfast?

    B. No, I don't want to disturb her. I'm sure _____

    _____. She _____

    _____ every day after breakfast.

7. A. Why don't you visit Barbara this afternoon?

B. No, I don't want to disturb her. I'm sure _____

_____ . She usually _____

_____ on Saturday afternoon.

F. LISTEN

Listen and fill in the blanks with the words you hear.

On the Airplane

Good afternoon. This is Captain Harris speaking. Our plane _____

in just a few minutes. Soon _____ over New York City, and _____

_____ to see the baseball stadium on your _____

and Central Park on your _____ . We'll be flying _____ the Atlantic

Ocean _____ three and a half hours. _____ , you'll be

_____ dinner, and after dinner _____ a movie.

_____ in San Juan at 8:35. The weather in San Juan

this evening is 70°F./21°C. and cloudy. _____ probably _____

when we get there.

In the Hospital

Now Mr. Jones, after your operation, _____ probably _____

_____ weak _____ . But don't worry! _____

_____ good care of you. Tomorrow _____

_____ in bed and resting _____ all day. The nurses _____

_____ your pulse and _____ pressure, and _____

_____ you _____ soup and juice. The day after tomorrow

_____ and _____ eat ice cream and yogurt. If

everything _____ O.K., _____ the hospital on Saturday. Do you

have _____ questions?

You'll Find Me

When you come _____ the restaurant, _____ who I am. _____

_____ dark glasses and a raincoat. _____ by myself

at a table _____ , and _____ a glass of

wine. _____ also _____ a cigarette and _____ a

newspaper. And _____ for you. _____

_____ me. Don't worry!

A. HELP

me	him	her	us	you	them
my	his	her	our	your	their
myself	himself	herself	ourselves	yourself	themselves
				yourselves	

1. _____*His*_____ family didn't help

   _____*him.*_____ He washed the kitchen

   floor by _____*himself.*_____

2. _____ mother didn't help

   _____. They baked this delicious

   bread by _____.

3. _____ parents usually help

   _____. But yesterday she studied

   by _____.

4. _____ friends can't help

   _____. We've got to paint the

   kitchen by _____.

5. Nobody is going to help

   _____. He has to fix _____

   car by _____.

6. I wrote this letter by _____.

   I'm glad _____ parents didn't help

   _____.

7. You don't have to paint the bathroom by _____. I really want to help _____.

8. Do you have any questions? I'll be glad to help _____. You don't have to do _____ homework by _____.

B. THE LOST UMBRELLA

| mine | his | hers | ours | yours | theirs |

A. I just found this umbrella in the closet. Is it _____yours?_____

B. No, it isn't _____. But it might be your friend Mary's. She always forgets things.

A. No, I'm sure it isn't _____. Her umbrella is red and this one is polka dot.

B. Do you think it might be Jeff's?

A. Jeff's?! No, it can't be _____. He doesn't have a polka dot umbrella!

B. How about Judy and Steve? Do you think it might be _____?

A. Not really. When they forget something, they always call right away.

B. Well, I don't know WHO forgot this umbrella, but WE certainly need one.

A. You're right. And if nobody asks for it soon, I guess it'll be _____!

C. SCRAMBLED SENTENCES

Unscramble the sentences.

1. when   sister   going   her   their   is   to   visit?

_____ _____ _____ _____ _____

_____ _____

2. are   brown   yours   these   gloves?

_____ _____ _____ _____ _____

3. he   give   wants   to   his   her   book

_____ _____ _____ _____ _____ _____

_____

4. we   send   her   him   address   didn't

_____ _____ _____ _____ _____ _____

5. we   ourselves   us   because   enjoyed   friends   our   with   were

_____ _____ _____ _____ _____ _____

_____ _____ _____ _____

6. he   dinner   cooks   his   by   because   help   himself   children
don't   him

_____ _____ _____ _____ _____ _____

_____ _____ _____ _____

7. they're   father's   writing   pen   their   with   because   theirs
they   lost

_____ _____ _____ _____ _____ _____

_____

D. NOISY NEIGHBORS

It's 4 a.m. and Michael can't fall asleep because his [neighbors / neighbor's] daughter [is playing / will be playing]

the piano. Last night she [played / is playing] the piano [until / for] six hours and Michael [won't be / wasn't] able

to [fall / fell] asleep. He's very upset because he studies [hardly / hard] all day and he needs to sleep

[at / in the] night. He doesn't know what to do.

It's midnight and I'm not asleep because the boy
| upstairs |
| downstairs |
is lifting
| heights. |
| weights. |
I don't

know why he isn't
| quietly |
| quieter |
! I don't like
| complain |
| to complain |
, but if that boy
| lifts |
| won't lift |
weights

again tomorrow night, I think I'll talk
| to |
| at |
the landlord or maybe even call the police!

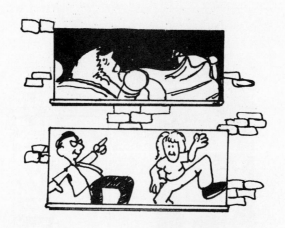

It's 2 a.m. and Helen can't fall asleep because
| her |
| hers |
downstairs neighbors
| were dancing. |
| are dancing. |

Last night they
| dance |
| danced |
| for |
| until |
3 a.m., and Helen is afraid that tomorrow they
| might |
| should |
dance

all night! The music is very
| loud |
| loudly |
, and Helen's neighbors are very
| noisy |
| noisily |
dancers. Helen is

upset. She doesn't like to complain, but she also doesn't like
| too tired |
| to be tired |
every morning. She

doesn't know what to do.

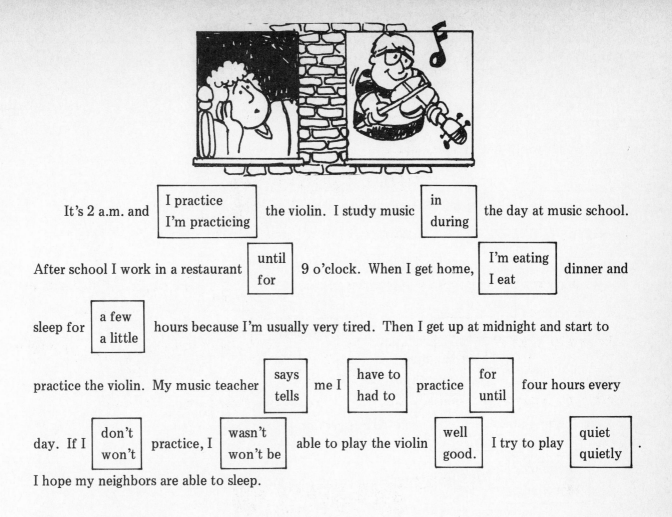

It's 2 a.m. and [I practice / I'm practicing] the violin. I study music [in / during] the day at music school.

After school I work in a restaurant [until / for] 9 o'clock. When I get home, [I'm eating / I eat] dinner and

sleep for [a few / a little] hours because I'm usually very tired. Then I get up at midnight and start to

practice the violin. My music teacher [says / tells] me I [have to / had to] practice [for / until] four hours every

day. If I [don't / won't] practice, I [wasn't / won't be] able to play the violin [well / good.] I try to play [quiet / quietly] .
I hope my neighbors are able to sleep.

E.   WHAT'S THE WORD?

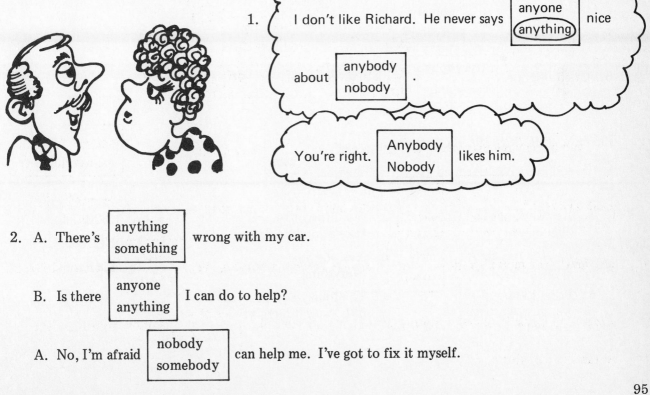

1.   I don't like Richard. He never says [anyone / (anything)] nice

about [anybody / nobody] .

You're right. [Anybody / Nobody] likes him.

2. A. There's [anything / something] wrong with my car.

   B. Is there [anyone / anything] I can do to help?

   A. No, I'm afraid [nobody / somebody] can help me. I've got to fix it myself.

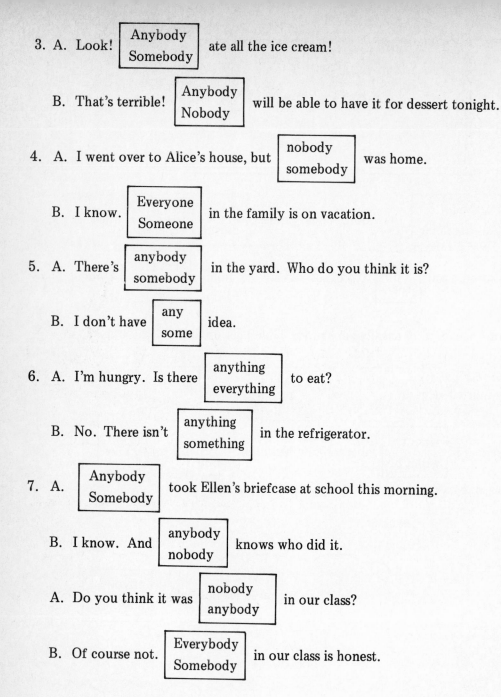

3. A. Look!
| Anybody |
| Somebody |
ate all the ice cream!

B. That's terrible!
| Anybody |
| Nobody |
will be able to have it for dessert tonight.

4. A. I went over to Alice's house, but
| nobody |
| somebody |
was home.

B. I know.
| Everyone |
| Someone |
in the family is on vacation.

5. A. There's
| anybody |
| somebody |
in the yard. Who do you think it is?

B. I don't have
| any |
| some |
idea.

6. A. I'm hungry. Is there
| anything |
| everything |
to eat?

B. No. There isn't
| anything |
| something |
in the refrigerator.

7. A.
| Anybody |
| Somebody |
took Ellen's briefcase at school this morning.

B. I know. And
| anybody |
| nobody |
knows who did it.

A. Do you think it was
| nobody |
| anybody |
in our class?

B. Of course not.
| Everybody |
| Somebody |
in our class is honest.

F.   LISTEN: *THE SCHOOL PICNIC*

Listen and put a circle around the correct answer.

1. a. No, we won't be
        able to go.

    b. No, I didn't enjoy
        myself very much.

    c. I don't know. My
        watch was broken.

2. a. No, I forgot to
        take a good book.

    b. Yes, she ate
        everything.

    c. The food was O.K.,
        but I wasn't hungry.

3. a. At 12:00.

    b. Until 12:30.

    c. In a few hours.

96

4. a. Because I was cleaning the apartment.

   b. Because I had to go home and take care of my younger brother.

   c. Because I won't be able to take my sister to the doctor.

5. a. I hope it was.

   b. I'm sure it is.

   c. We'll just have to wait and see.

G. YOU DECIDE: *WHAT'S MR. SMITH SAYING?*

A. Hello. May I speak to Mr. Smith?

B. ....

A. Yes, there's something wrong with my TV, and I need a TV repairman who can come over and fix it.

B. ....

A. No, it's a black-and-white TV.

B. ....

A. I don't know what's wrong. It just doesn't work at all.

B. ....

A. I live at 156 Grove Street in Centerville.

B. ....

A. Drive down State Street and turn left. My house is the last one on the right.

B. ....

A. Not really. I'm afraid I won't be home tomorrow at 2:00. Can you come at any other time?

B. ....

A. That's fine. I'll see you then.

B. Good-bye.

A. Good-bye.

A. Would you like to go to the movies with me this afternoon?

B. ....

A. That's too bad. Do you think Jack might be able to go?

B. ....

A. That's right. I forgot. He's always busy on Friday afternoon. How about Alice and Jane? They usually like to go to the movies.

B. ....

A. Well, I hope they enjoy themselves. Do you think Sally might want to go?

B. ....

A. Poor Sally. She always has problems with her house. How about Ted?

B. ....

A. Really? That's terrible. Nobody told me! How did he hurt himself?

B. ....

A. When you see him, tell him I'm very sorry. Well, I guess I won't go to the movies tonight. Maybe I'll stay home and study.

I. WHAT'S THE 🔘RIGHT/WRITE WORD?

Put a circle around the correct word.

1. Last weak / **(week)** he was too **(weak)** / week to get out of bed.

2. | Their / They're | going to take | their / they're | children to the zoo.

3. Last night I | ate / eight | | ate / eight | cookies.

4. You're | right. / write. | I should | right / write | a letter to my grandmother.

5. Did you | hear / here | me? Please put your umbrella over | hear. / here. |

6. | Wear / Where | are my sister's gloves? I want to | wear / where | them.

7. | You're / Your | late. | You're / Your | uncle arrived a few minutes ago.

8. Last week my son | read / red | a book about a little | read / red | train.

9. The woman with the yellow | flour / flower | in her hair is buying a five-pound bag of | flour / flower. |

10. | Our / Hour | plane should be here in an | our. / hour. |

11. I'm going to buy a | pear / pair | for lunch and a | pear / pair | of new shoes for the party tonight.

12. Do you | know / no | my friend Carl? | Know, / No, | I don't.

13. Let's | buy / by | some candles and eat dinner | buy / by | candlelight.

14. I bought | for / four | birthday presents | for / four | my mother.

15. | Too / Two | desserts are | too / two | many desserts for me.

16. There's a big | hole / whole | in my piece of | hole / whole | wheat bread!

A. Complete the sentences.

Ex. Will you be home this evening?
Yes, I will.   (watch TV)

_____ *I'll be watching TV.* _____

1. Will your parents be busy this afternoon?
Yes, they will.   (paint)

_____ the garage.

2. Will your sister be home at 4:00?
Yes, she will.   (study)

_____

3. Will your brother be home at 5:00?
Yes, he will.   (practice)

_____ the piano.

4. Will you and your wife be busy this
afternoon?
Yes, we will.   (take care of)

_____ our
grandchildren.

5. Will you be at the office tonight?
Yes, I will.   (work)

_____ late.

B. Complete the questions.

Ex. When _____ *will you be getting married?* _____
We'll be getting married next summer.

1. How late _____?
She'll be working until 8:00.

2. How much longer _____?
I'll be reading for a few more hours.

3. How soon _____?
He'll be coming tomorrow morning.

4. How far _____?
They'll be driving until they reach Tokyo.

5. How long _____?
We'll be staying in New York until Sunday.

C. Put a circle around the correct answer.

1. My doctor says I must eat [less / fewer] butter,

[less / fewer] eggs, and [less / fewer] fatty meat.

2. I [mustn't / don't have to] study tonight, but I think
I should.

3. Mary [mustn't / doesn't have to] eat too [much / many]
salt because she has problems with her
blood pressure.

4. If you want to get a job in Mr. Wilson's office,
you must speak English and Spanish, but you

[mustn't / don't have to] type very well.

5. We'll be working at the bank [for / until]
September.

6. She'll be playing the violin [for / until] a few
more minutes.

7. We finished our dinner [at / until] 6:00.

8. I'll be going to Paris [at / in] a few days.

9. I have to go to the supermarket. There isn't
[anything / something] in the refrigerator.

10. If you look in the yellow pages, I'm sure

you'll find [anybody / somebody] who can fix your

TV.

11. [Anyone / Someone] ate all the yogurt in the

refrigerator.

12. This is his sandwich. It isn't [my / mine] .

13. I don't think this is [their / theirs] book, but it

might be [her / hers] .

14. We gave [her / his] our address.

D. LISTEN

Listen and fill in the missing words.

On the Bus

Good morning. This is your bus driver,
Jim Smith, speaking. I'm glad

_____ with us on this
special weekend visit to New York City.

_____ in just a few minutes

and _____ in New York City
at noon, in time for a delicious lunch at the
Park Avenue Cafe. After lunch

_____ The United Nations,

and in the evening _____
dinner at one of New York's finest restaurants.

Don't forget! _____ at the
Fifth Avenue Hotel across the street from the
beautiful Museum of Modern Art. I'm sure

you're all going to enjoy _____

very much. If I can do _____

to help you, _____